BEHIND THE HAPPY SMILES
LURKED DARK SECRETS . . .
AND A DEVIOUS, DANGEROUS MIND

DUANE—A hardworking "nice guy" whose fatal mistake may have been to marry the wrong woman.

SANDY—A pretty, petite, blue-eyed blonde who seemed sweet as sugar until it came to men . . . and being a catalyst for trouble.

SALLIE—Sandy's younger sister, whose friendly call on her family would leave her facing the prospect of a terrifying death.

CHAD—Sallie's baby son, who didn't have a chance.

SHERRIE—Duane and Sandy's daughter, who innocently ate a bowl of cereal that slowly and horribly began to kill her . . .

JIM—Sandy's high school sweetheart, who found that becoming her husband could provoke even a sane man to violence.

STEVE—Sandy's ex-boyfriend, the mild-mannered aspiring veterinarian whom everybody loved . . . and nobody really knew.

QUANTITY SALES

Most Dell books are available at special quantity discounts when purchased in bulk by corporations, organizations, or groups. Special imprints, messages, and excerpts can be produced to meet your needs. For more information, write to: Dell Publishing, 1540 Broadway, New York, NY 10036. Attention: Director, Special Markets.

INDIVIDUAL SALES

Are there any Dell books you want but cannot find in your local stores? If so, you can order them directly from us. You can get any Dell book currently in print. For a complete up-to-date listing of our books and information on how to order, write to: Dell Readers Service, Box DR, 1540 Broadway, New York, NY 10036.

TOXIC LOVE

The Chilling True Story of Twisted Passion in the "Murder by Cancer" Case

Tomas Guillen

A Dell Book

Published by
Dell Publishing
a division of
Bantam Doubleday Dell Publishing Group, Inc.
1540 Broadway
New York, New York 10036

Copyright © 1995 by Tomas Guillen

ISBN: 0-440-21793-8

Printed in the United States of America

Published simultaneously in Canada

June 1995

10 9 8 7 6 5 4 3 2 1
OPM

*To Susan and our children:
Natalie, Phillip, Anne. With all
my love. Thank you for enduring
my absence during the writing of
this book.*

ACKNOWLEDGMENTS

No project is ever the work of one individual; numerous people contribute many hours of their professional and personal time.

My special thanks to former Omaha Police Department Chief Richard R. Andersen; Lieutenant Foster Burchard; Detective K. G. Miller; and Deputy County Prosecutor Sam Cooper. They opened their files to enable me to map out the investigation and prosecution.

My thanks, also, to Dr. Robert L. Frerichs; Dr. Luther A. Frerichs; Tamara A. Turner, director of hospital library services for Children's Hospital and Medical Center in Seattle, Washington; and Sandy Freeman of *The Seattle Times* library. The doctors provided valuable assistance in interpreting medical records, while Turner and Freeman helped locate hard-to-find research.

I also would like to express my appreciation to the Nebraska State Patrol and the Nebraska State Penitentiary for their cooperation.

I am grateful to my editor, Steve Ross, and my agent, Jane Dystel, for their guidance. *Seattle Times* copy editor Emmett Murray also assisted in reading and critiquing the manuscript. Bruce McKim of *The Seattle Times'* photography department prepared all the photographs.

My gratitude to Dean Suing, Ann Benson, Karen Frerichs, Sarah Frerichs, Genevieve Frerichs, Don Carson, and Nick Provenza for their friendship, enthusiasm, and moral support.

Words cannot express my debt to the woman who raised me, my grandmother, "Mama."

AUTHOR'S NOTE

This is a true story. The real names of those involved have been used. Most of the dialogue comes from police and court documents or the participants. At times, the dialogue was reconstructed from interviews with numerous persons familiar with the events.

Contents

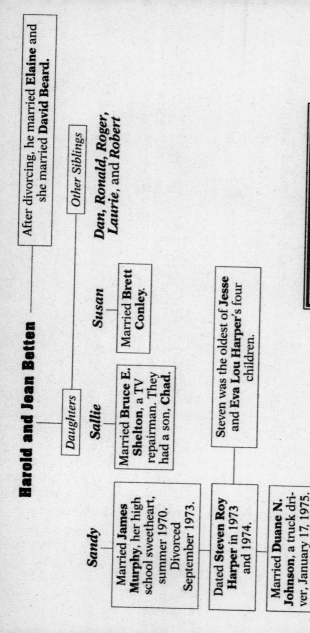

Harold and Jean Betten

After divorcing, he married Elaine and she married **David Beard**.

Daughters

Other Siblings

Dan, Ronald, Roger, Laurie, and *Robert*

Sandy

Married **James Murphy**, her high school sweetheart, summer 1970. Divorced September 1973.

Dated **Steven Roy Harper** in 1973 and 1974.

Married **Duane N. Johnson**, a truck driver, January 17, 1975. Two children: **Sherrie** and **Michael**.

Sallie

Married **Bruce E. Shelton**, a TV repairman. They had a son, **Chad**.

Steven was the oldest of Jesse and Eva Lou Harper's four children.

Susan

Married **Brett Conley**.

THE FAMILIES

Book One
THE ENIGMA

One

AFTER A LATE NIGHT of cards, Sandy and Duane Johnson slept in. Two-year-old Sherrie was the first to get up, shortly after nine. By then, the thick fog that hid the city at sunrise had burned off, unveiling a beautiful Indian-summer day that promised to be one of those humid Midwest scorchers.

While Sherrie ate a small bowl of cereal, her father shuffled sleepily into the kitchen and poured himself a large glass of milk. His face wrinkled up like a prune.

"This milk tastes funny," Duane complained.

His wife smelled the opening of the gallon jug and looked inside.

"It's not curdled or anything," Sandy said. "It looks fine to me."

"Something's wrong with it," Duane insisted, setting the glass down on the table. "It tastes real funny."

To avert an argument so early on a gorgeous Sunday morning, Sandy grabbed the gallon of milk and emptied it into the sink. That satisfied her husband, a happy-go-lucky man who rarely grumbled about anything. Duane Johnson was twenty-four and the family's only breadwinner. He drove a truck for Hendrickson Equipment & Welding Supply Co., delivering industrial gases and equipment throughout the Midwest.

Still sleeping were the couple's infant son, Michael, and Sandy's sister, Susan Conley, who was nineteen and nine months pregnant. She'd been staying in the Johnsons' spare bedroom about a month, since she'd split up with her husband during a bad quarrel.

After breakfast, Sherrie complained of a stomachache, but at 10:30 she accompanied her mother to K mart anyway.

Duane stayed home to paint the outside of their modest three-bedroom home on Fontenelle Boulevard. The shoe box house with the A-frame roof stood amid a cluster of tall cottonwood trees next to a large vacant lot. It was hard to believe it contained three bedrooms, in addition to a bathroom, a kitchen, and a living room.

Small or not, it was the Johnsons' dream home. They'd bought it only eight months before, partly because it sat in a quiet, well-groomed neighborhood in the far north end of Omaha, miles from downtown and the city's business districts.

As the largest city in Nebraska, Omaha served as a national center for telemarketing companies that promoted and sold products by phone, and the headquarters for over thirty-five insurance firms. Most of all, Omaha was home to a compassionate people and Father Flanagan's Boys Town. The Catholic priest founded the home for boys in 1917 on the creed: "No Boy Is a Bad Boy."

To many, Omaha was Main Street America, a bastion of wholesome middle-class values. But on this blisteringly hot day, there was evil in the city. Duane Johnson and his little daughter Sherrie didn't know it, but while they were walking and talking, they were dying. Something was eating away at their bodies.

While Duane used a wide brush to turn his blue house a tulip yellow, Sandy's father and stepmother arrived. Harold and Elaine Betten were on their way home from church and dropped by to return a lawn mower they'd borrowed. Elaine Betten was known for telling corny jokes. Whenever someone asked her to spell her last name, she'd laugh: "Like we bet ten at the races, but we don't go. There we go again."

"If you're real busy," Harold shouted at Duane, who was halfway up a ladder, "we won't stay."

"No, no," Duane said with a grin. "It will give me a good excuse to quit painting. It's so hot out here."

Inside, the Bettens boiled water and fixed themselves coffee. Duane drank a cool ale. The couple indulged in a second cup of coffee with a piece of pecan pie before deciding to leave.

"Did you notice Duane?" Elaine asked her husband in the car.

"What do you mean?"

"He was talking in slow motion," she said. "Seriously, he was having trouble pronouncing his words."

If he'd overheard this remark, Duane Johnson would have been surprised. He thought he was fine. He went back to his paint can and brush.

He was still on his ladder at noon when Sandy unexpectedly returned home from the supermarket.

"What's wrong?" asked Duane.

"Sherrie keeps throwing up," Sandy said. "She threw up all over the store. I had to leave the groceries in the basket."

As Sandy described the scene at the store, Duane abruptly threw up as well. It must be the flu, he decided. Suddenly Duane felt rotten all over. Both father and daughter went straight to bed.

That Sunday, Sallie and Bruce Shelton had risen at dawn to shampoo their carpets at their attractive brick rambler on Sharon Drive a few minutes away from the home of Duane and Sandy Johnson. Sallie was Sandy Johnson's younger sister. Sallie and Bruce planned a busy day and were eager to be out and about town. By nightfall they, too, would face the prospect of a terrifying death.

After arranging and rearranging the furniture in their home, the Sheltons scooped up their spunky eleven-month-old son, Chad, and buckled him into the family car, along with plenty of diapers and baby bottles. They planned to be gone all day.

"Where to first?" asked Bruce as he backed the car out of the driveway.

"The Nebraska Furniture Mart, of course," Sallie said.

Bruce wasn't surprised. In the months before Chad's birth, the Sheltons had spent almost all of their free time in the store trying to decide how to decorate the new arrival's room. Sallie and Bruce knew the store so well they might as well have owned it. The store was one of the state's largest furniture outlets, occupying almost an entire block off of Dodge Street, Omaha's main east-west thoroughfare.

At the store, Sallie and Bruce went straight to the light fixture section and bought a pair of stylish lamps they'd been eyeing for some time. Anxious to show off their latest purchase, Sallie and Bruce drove over to see Sandy and Duane. The two sisters saw each other frequently.

Both Sandy and Sallie were petite and pretty. Sandy possessed piercing blue eyes and wavy blond hair, like her father. Sallie took after her mother, a brunette with warm brown eyes.

While the sisters resembled each other in looks, they were opposites in most other ways. While Sandy seemed satisfied to live the life of a housewife, Sallie Shelton was a career woman. She sustained her family and was nearing a promotion to a supervisory position at Mutual of Omaha, the giant insurance company. Her nontraditional role in marriage was at the forefront of a trend soon to become commonplace in relationships. Bruce, a tall, muscular man who favored a mustache and goatee, repaired television sets for Professional Electronics, a small south end business. He had a steady wage, but his job lacked potential, prestige. The marriage worked, though, and that's what mattered.

By the time the Sheltons arrived at the Johnsons' about 3 P.M., their clothes were soaked with sweat from the sweltering 91-degree heat.

"You're welcome to come in, but I have to warn you that Duane and Sherrie are sick," Sandy told her sister at the front door. "I think they have the flu."

"We'll just stay for a few minutes," Sallie said.

Sandy served everyone cool beverages, then

went into the bedrooms to check on her husband and daughter. They were taking turns in the bathroom, throwing up.

After quenching their thirst and displaying the new fixtures, the Sheltons waved good-bye and headed to their main destination, a birthday party for Bruce's niece.

Plenty of cake and ice cream were served at the party, but not much else, prompting the Sheltons to stop at a Taco Real on their way home. They loved Mexican food. As the sun inched toward the horizon just before six that evening, the family looked forward to watching *60 Minutes*.

Sallie felt queasy while unloading the car, and upon walking in the house vomited. She thought little of it since she'd always suffered from a nervous stomach. After deciding to eat the tacos anyway, she fed her son bits of the burned hamburger filling. The tacos tasted funny, though. Actually, they tasted terrible and she threw them away. Bruce did the same with his.

A short time later, Chad threw up. There was something about the way he vomited that bothered Sallie. It wasn't just a normal baby's spit-up; his whole body trembled. Now that she thought about it, her son had been uncomfortable since early afternoon. The lethargy she had taken to be tiredness, in retrospect, may have been the beginning of an illness. Maybe it

wasn't what they had eaten; maybe the Johnsons' flu had come home with them.

Cuddling her precious son and stroking his
moon-shaped face, she fervently wished he
could talk and tell her what was wrong. Gazing
at Chad, she realized her own body ached. Her
stomach hurt so much she went to bed before
60 Minutes even came on. Chad normally slept
by himself, but, tonight, his mother tucked him
in beside her.

At nine that evening, loud gagging awakened Sallie. It was Bruce. Vomit was caught in
his throat and it seemed forever before he
caught his breath. Within seconds, Bruce
gagged again and gasped for an ounce of air.
With each vomiting spell, she heard the pungent liquid splash all over the bathroom. She
desperately wanted to get out of bed to help
him, but she couldn't. During her brief sleep,
something drained her of all energy.

To Bruce, the vomiting fits came so violently
they felt like his stomach was exorcising something evil instead of simply spitting out a piece
of food that disagreed with it. His whole body
shook like an old motor out of tune. Once the
vomiting ceased, Bruce could hardly move; he
had to lie on his back on the bathroom floor to
rest before dragging himself to bed. Sallie and
Bruce tried sleeping, but they ached too much.
Chad slept restlessly.

Although the Sheltons believed they were
merely suffering from the Johnsons' flu or pos-

sibly a bout of routine food poisoning, they worried about their infant son. Bruce, especially, found it hard to understand how Chad's body could endure a fraction of what he and his wife were going through. He couldn't recall ever feeling so sick, so physically wasted. And as he lay awake, his head started throbbing with excruciating pain. What was going on? What was making them so sick?

To convince himself it wasn't a bad dream, Bruce telephoned his own sister about eleven o'clock. She blamed it all on the tacos. That comforted Bruce, but it failed to completely erase his concern. He called Dr. R. David Glover, Chad's physician, at home and described Chad's symptoms.

"Sounds like food poisoning," Glover guessed. "Let's see how he does. If you don't feel he's gotten any better by morning, bring him to the clinic."

Bruce returned to bed and told Sallie what Glover had said. There wasn't much that could be done for ordinary food poisoning, according to Glover. Still, for most of the rest of the night, Sallie and Bruce vomited violently off and on. Each time, their stomachs ached more than the previous time.

Two

DUANE JOHNSON'S ENTIRE BODY hurt so much—in every bone and muscle—that he didn't report for work. And his head ached so badly, he devoured aspirin six at a time. The aspirin did nothing to ease his pain. Sherrie, too, complained of pain racking her tiny body. She moaned constantly. Neither she nor Duane could eat without vomiting.

Sandy spent all day caring for her husband and daughter and wiping vomit off the bathroom floor. She couldn't clean it up fast enough.

That night, Duane and Sherrie again had trouble sleeping. To help the others get some rest, Duane decided he and Sherrie should sleep together in the main bedroom. Sandy slept with her infant son.

* * *

Meanwhile, a few blocks away, Bruce Shelton felt a little better, but his midsection and head still hurt. He hated missing work, over anything, so he forced himself out of bed to his job. Sallie could just manage a weak good-bye.

All day, she stayed in bed, getting up only to care for her baby Chad, who was as tired and droopy as his mother. Chad normally ate baby fruit, crackers, bananas, and milk. Today, a taste or two of the fruit was all she could get him to eat, along with some water. Sallie ate nothing, mostly out of fear of throwing up. Chad cried constantly when he wasn't sleeping.

In the evening, Sallie and Bruce lounged around the house, having little strength to do anything else, even call relatives.

With each passing hour, their usually active infant became more listless and, at times, could barely lift his head from his pillow. Before going to bed, his parents agreed to take him to the hospital if he didn't improve the next day.

Tuesday morning, September 12

The following day, Duane and his daughter felt a bit better. Still, they were unable to keep any food down.

Duane started developing nosebleeds. Every so often, big red drops plopped on the bed sheets, like a leaky faucet. They came more frequently as the morning wore on. Sherrie did not bleed, but her skin turned a dull white.

Concerned, Sandy called the Northwest Clinic and made an appointment for Wednesday afternoon with Dr. R. David Glover, the same doctor Bruce Shelton had called Sunday night.

Only five minutes from Immanuel Medical Center, the clinic was in a large, old two-story house with a brick veneer. The upstairs served as an apartment and had its separate entrance. The downstairs had been remodeled with a reception area and nine examining rooms. Six days a week, Monday through Saturday, Glover and his two partners treated patients between visits to Immanuel to follow up on the more severe cases and to deliver babies. For after-hours emergencies, the receptionist gave patients the physicians' home number.

The Johnsons and Sheltons had been visiting the Northwest Clinic for their health needs for a couple of years and most always were treated by Glover. Both families considered Glover their doctor.

Glover had a much different perspective: To him, the Johnsons and the Sheltons were indistinguishable faces in the waiting room. There was nothing unique about them; they were just like the hundreds who came in every year or so for a fever or a stubborn headache. In fact, Glover saw so many patients at the clinic—especially walk-ins—that he had trouble recalling the medical histories of the Johnsons and Sheltons. He couldn't even remember if he'd delivered their children, although he guessed he probably had. He had no idea that the two families were related.

In truth, Glover appeared a bit ambivalent about the Johnsons and Sheltons. To him, they were not really *his* patients: They were patients of the clinic, the family practice.

On the same Tuesday morning, Sallie Shelton awoke at 5 A.M. and after glancing at her son, she shook her husband: "Bruce, Chad doesn't look any better. Take him to the hospital."

Sallie struggled to help get Chad ready. She was not going to the hospital. She hated to think of her baby without her; yet, realistically, she knew she could not function. She was sure her sickness was food poisoning, not the flu. Still, it was difficult to believe food poisoning— a few lousy tacos—could make anyone so sick.

Bruce drove his son to Immanuel Medical Center, a tall white private hospital at the end of North 72nd Street in North Omaha. As he carried him into the emergency room at six forty-five, Chad felt like a limp rag. A nurse took the boy from Bruce while he provided information in an admissions process that seemed interminable.

No, Chad had never been severely ill. No, Chad had no history of exposure to a communicable disease. No, he had had no vaccinations in the last month. Allergies? None. Family medical history? Negative for bleeding disorders, TB, epilepsy and heart disease. Mother? Where's the child's mother? Bruce explained that his wife was also ill and too weak to venture out of the house. The hospital employee writing down the information nodded understandingly and encouraged him to keep his spouse home.

By the time the admission paperwork was completed, it was close to nine o'clock in the morning. At that point, an emergency nurse turned to Bruce and smiled: "Go on. We'll take care of him." Bruce left for work.

While emergency room doctors ordered X rays and blood work for routine laboratory tests, nurses readied a crib for Chad on the fifth floor in the pediatrics–young adult unit of the hospital. An Iowa native, Lynda Rummel, supervised the forty-one-room unit with the help of twenty-five nurses, who were always extremely busy at this time of year treating children with bad colds or the flu. By 1 P.M., the baby had made his way up to Rummel's floor. Although suspected of suffering only from the "crud"—gastroenteritis—Chad was placed in room 511 alone.

"He was put in a room by himself because we didn't know what he had," recalled Rummel years later. "He seemed like a normal, healthy baby. He was a little fussy but his color and vitals were normal. Our goal was to keep an eye on him, give him plenty of fluids."

Rummel planned to assign Nurse Pamela Zyck, who worked the three-to-eleven shift, to care for the sick child. Zyck was only twenty and relatively fresh out of nurses' training, but she was especially suited for infants. She had a knack for observing a child's eyes and movements and translating her perceptions into medical diagnosis. Pediatrics units cherished that ability, because most of their patients were too young to talk.

Meanwhile, while making his morning rounds at Immanuel, Glover learned from the staff that one of the clinic's patients had been admitted. He went up to the fifth floor to see Chad. Everything pointed to a simple case of the flu—not food poisoning—but the patient's eyes looked slightly jaundiced, a yellowish tinge indicative of possible liver or blood system problems. To guard against infection, he asked the staff to give Chad ampicillin, an antibiotic.

Tuesday evening, September 12

That evening, Sallie and Bruce went to see their son at Immanuel, hoping he would be well enough to smile a bit. Bruce attempted to dissuade his wife from leaving home, because she had not eaten all day, for the second day in a row. But Sallie needed to see her baby; she yearned to hold him. As they tiptoed into his room—painted an ugly orange and red—tears welled up in their eyes. To them, their son looked worse.

Nurse Zyck and the rest of the night shift agreed the boy appeared a little more uncomfortable, but there wasn't much they could do. He had the flu, they were sure.

To Sallie and Bruce, Chad was much too sick to be suffering from the flu. At 10:30 P.M., the couple walked out of the hospital dejected and bewildered. At the time, no one knew enough to question them about *their* symptoms to ascertain what might be wrong with them or their son.

Before going off duty at 11 P.M. Nurse Zyck turned in her report:

"↑ Temp, ↓ appetite, vomiting. No diarrhea. Napping @ intervals. Listless. Parents here this P.M. Crying @ intervals. Pulling @ L ear while crying. Mother states he has been doing this for a few days."

As the night wore on, however, Chad, Duane, and Sherrie grew sicker and sicker.

Wednesday morning, September 13

Duane Johnson awoke before dawn with large blood clots all over the whites of his eyes and blood oozing from his gums. He could hardly stand to look at himself in the mirror: His face resembled that of a bloody creature from a late-night horror show.

Sandy offered to cancel a dentist appointment that morning, but her husband insisted she keep it.

"I'll be all right," mumbled Duane on his way back to the bedroom.

But he wasn't all right. He couldn't stay awake. When he did manage to open his eyes, the light rays stung like straight pins. He had to squint to see.

Several miles away, at Immanuel Medical Center, the graveyard shift began noticing a drastic change in Chad Shelton's condition about 3 A.M. He started getting more lethargic and turning purple. Bruises covered the skin around his eyes, stomach, palms, and feet.

Rummel knew something was badly wrong when a staff nurse called her at home about 6 A.M. Rummel was awake, but still in bed.

"Did you see this little Shelton boy when he came in yesterday?" asked the nurse.

"Yes," Rummel said.

The nurse described Chad's symptoms. "Was he like that?"

"No, he wasn't."

"He's been changing all night, but he looks worse than he looked two hours ago," the nurse told Rummel. "He looks *much* worse. I'm very concerned about him."

"I'll be right there," Rummel said. "In the meantime, check his vitals and call Dr. Glover."

Rolling up her long blond hair into a tight bun to conceal it under her nurse's cap, Rummel wondered what had gone wrong with Chad. In just a matter of hours, his condition had completely flip-flopped. It was puzzling. She dressed and quickly drove the two miles from her apartment to the hospital.

On her arrival, Rummel overheard the nurse on the phone with Glover. Rummel shed her coat at the nurses' station and walked briskly to room 511. The boy's coloring was so "awful" it scared Rummel. She'd never had a patient under ten die on her.

"Chad?" she called out, bending over the boy. *"Chad?"* No response. She picked up his small arm. It dropped like a floppy doll's. He just lay there, as in a deep sleep. She ran back to the nurses' station.

"We need to do something right away," she thought. "He needs help."

By then, the nurse was off the phone and acting on Glover's request to contact Dr. John Schiffbauer, a specialist in pediatrics based at Children's Hospital, also in Omaha.

Schiffbauer hurried to Immanuel. After one look at the boy, he ordered a variety of blood tests, including a count of the child's platelets, microscopic disk-shaped structures that help in blood clotting. From this point forward, Chad was under Schiffbauer's care.

Schiffbauer consulted neurologist Clifford Danneel, who suggested a spinal tap to determine if Chad suffered from meningitis, a serious infectious disease of the brain and spinal cord that caused children to become unresponsive. The disease was lethal if not caught early.

At 9 A.M., Danneel slowly inserted a long needle between the vertebrae in Chad's back and drew out spinal fluid. An examination of the liquid with the naked eye showed it to be clear and colorless, indicating the absence of infection or disease. To be certain, though, the doctor had the fluid rushed to the laboratory in the basement for a chemical analysis.

"I'm not really sure what's going on here," Schiffbauer admitted to Rummel, "but it could be Reye's syndrome. I don't really know, yet."

At the time, a horrendous number of Reye's syndrome cases had swept the nation. The rare disorder afflicted children given aspirin during a viral illness. Reye's syndrome usually results in death, but brain damage frequently occurs even if the child survives.

After a brief discussion, Schiffbauer and Danneel decided to move Chad to Children's Hospital, where he could be treated by physicians trained in various pediatric specialties. Rummel asked a nurse to contact the boy's parents.

At home, Sallie's weak body tightened on answering the phone. She'd been dreading the call: Chad had worsened and was being transferred to Children's Hospital. She and Bruce should go directly there. The urgent message melted away Sallie's own aches and pains. She called Bruce.

Rummel and another nurse rolled a bed carrying Chad onto the elevator and rode to the lobby. There, the child was gently placed into an ambulance for the ten-minute trip to Children's. A nurse climbed in with him. Rummel stayed behind to look after her other small patients.

"Oh my God," thought Rummel, trying to hold back tears. She was single with no children, but she adored kids. "What's wrong with this boy? Does he have leukemia? Reye's syndrome?"

She'd never seen a patient go downhill so fast without a prolonged rise in temperature or changes in other vital signs. Chad's condition bothered Rummel terribly. She kept hoping whatever he had was reversible, but the doctors had no idea of what they were trying to reverse. Whatever was happening to Chad was happening so fast that medicine could not keep up with it.

On arriving at Children's emergency room about 10 A.M., Chad appeared to be in a coma. An intensive care unit physician ordered "the works." The staff inserted an I.V. into a vein to give the child dextrose water and a tube into his lungs to help him breathe. His brain, apparently, was not telling him to breathe often enough.

The intensive care doctor called in another

neurologist to find out why Chad continued to slide. As the two doctors examined him, the boy's limbs started twitching, a clear sign of a brain seizure. The neurologist attempted to administer a simple muscle-strength test, but the baby's arms and legs stiffened oddly, into a position known as decerebrate posturing. That condition implies brain injury, particularly to the part of the brain that makes a person aware of his surroundings. To help stop the brain seizures, doctors gave Chad Decadron, a cortisone-type steroid aimed at decreasing swelling in the brain.

A nurse noticed Chad's skin turning yellow, a common sign of liver failure. The doctors ordered the emergency room staff to contact Immanuel's laboratory technologists to determine what, if anything, was learned from blood and platelet tests conducted prior to the baby's transfer. The results astonished physicians at both hospitals.

According to the tests, Chad's platelet count was 19,000, far below a normal count of 140,000 to 440,000. Spontaneous bleeding occurred at 19,000. The patient's blood-sugar test also came back low, 11. It should have been closer to 80. And his blood ammonia was about 300. It wasn't supposed to be more than 50. The blood-sugar and blood-ammonia tests were further proof Chad's liver was failing, since one of the liver's primary jobs is to keep the blood sugar in a normal range and help in removing ammonia from the blood.

While nurses frantically gave Chad transfusions of red blood cells to allow his body to carry more oxygen, he coughed up blood. Now, the boy was bleeding internally, apparently from the lack of platelets, and other abnormal coagulation factors. Doctors ordered a nasogastric-suction tube placed into his stomach to suck out the blood. After inserting the tube, the nurses resumed giving him red blood cells via an I.V. A short time later, they added platelets to the I.V. to try to stop the internal bleeding.

By then, nurses were pumping a variety of medications into Chad through other I.V.'s: Decadron to keep his brain from swelling; phenobarbital to inhibit seizure activity; isoproterenol to maintain his blood pressure; and vitamin K to prompt the liver to produce the factors that help blood clot. The urgency of the situation appeared to justify administering the vitamin K through an I.V., a rarity because of the risk of causing cardiac arrest. Customarily, vitamin K was injected into a patient's muscle.

As morning turned to afternoon, the doctors increasingly worried about Chad's brain. Would he sustain brain damage? They decided to keep track of his brain's activity with a bolt intracranial pressure monitor. A nurse shaved a spot on the baby's right-front head and a doctor drilled a tiny hole through the skull. A surgeon then carefully screwed in the bolt. The monitor had been in Chad only a short time when bleeding developed around the instrument. Doctors waited a moment—hoping the bleeding would stop—but it persisted. The monitor was removed.

Throughout the day, Sallie and Bruce solemnly observed the parade of medical personnel going in and out of their son's room at Children's. When doctors wanted to try another procedure, they'd ask the couple to leave. But Chad's health deteriorated with each successive attempt to make him well. Their son, essentially, had been unresponsive most of the day and doctors considered him in a stage 4 coma, with 5 being the worst.

Each time Sallie and Bruce returned to Chad's room, after stepping out for the hospital staff, they were stunned by what they saw. There was this little body—just over two feet five inches long—with transparent tubes sticking out of everywhere. One I.V. penetrated his right groin. A second one entered at the right wrist. A third went in through the left ankle. Three other plastic tubes disappeared into his body cavities: one to help him breathe, one to drain his bladder, and one to suction blood from his stomach.

Within a few more hours, Chad's heart rate would fluctuate erratically, making everyone uneasy. In the irreverent words of a medical intern, he was "circling the drain."

Wednesday afternoon, September 13

Duane Johnson and his daughter Sherrie were about to climb in the tub to clean up for their visit to the clinic when the phone rang. It was Sallie and Bruce calling to say Chad was in the hospital, on the critical list, suffering from some unknown illness. Duane could tell they'd been crying. The information about Chad frightened Duane; the idea of a child being gravely ill reminded him of Sherrie's condition. Her symptoms weren't as severe as Duane's, but she was still very sick. But Duane had no idea that he and Sherrie might be suffering from the same thing that ailed Chad.

Still, for the first time, the two families became aware of each other's ordeals, although not in any great detail.

About 3 P.M., Sandy and Duane and their two children went to Glover's office. Duane and Sherrie's symptoms baffled the doctor, but he dismissed them with instructions to notify him if Duane's bleeding continued into Friday.

To Glover, Duane was suffering from a rather routine nosebleed.

Unfortunately, Glover did not know that Duane and Sherrie were related to Chad, and the Johnsons apparently did not volunteer the information. As a result, no one at that time saw the deadly connection between the families' looming tragedies.

Exasperated, the Johnsons returned home

to continue living their own separate nightmare.

Wednesday night, September 13

While sitting in the living room watching television that night, Duane's rather routine nosebleed got a lot worse. He sneezed and blood
gushed from his nose. Sandy ran to the phone
and called Glover at home. The doctor politely
asked that she call him back in twenty minutes
if the bleeding continued.

Sandy didn't know what to do, so she called
her mother, Jean Beard: "Mom, Duane's real
sick. I don't know what's wrong with him."

"Well, what hurts?" Jean asked.

"Everything," Sandy said, "and he's got
blood in his eyes and mouth. It doesn't look
right."

"Blood? From what?"

"I don't know. He's scary."

Jean and her husband, Dave Beard, hurried
over. Duane sat stooped in a living room chair
with a blanket around his shoulders like an old
beggar.

Dave took one look at his son-in-law and
gasped: "My God, Duane, you look like shit.
What's the matter with you?"

"I don't know what's wrong with me," mur-
mured Duane, who appeared to be crying, but it
was hard to tell with all the blood in his eyes.

He looked up at his mother-in-law wistfully: "Mom, do something, please. I'm sick. Help me."

Suddenly, Duane sneezed again and released another unbelievable stream of blood. It was unlike any other nosebleed. It went everywhere: on shoes, on the carpet. He bled so much he had to drop to his knees over the toilet to have a basin large enough to catch the flood.

Again, Sandy contacted Glover. This time, he agreed to meet Duane in the emergency room of the Immanuel Medical Center, the same hospital that had treated Chad before he was transferred to Children's Hospital earlier that day. Glover halted the unusual bleeding by packing Duane's nose.

But almost as soon as the Johnsons returned home, they faced yet *another* crisis: Susan Conley, Sandy's pregnant sister, went into labor. The family went right back to Immanuel Medical Center, where she delivered a baby boy a few hours later. Susan, too, was Glover's patient, but an associate delivered the baby.

Thursday morning, September 14

About 4 A.M., Chad's vital signs went awry. His heart rate accelerated wildly, then plummeted. He could barely breathe. Blood-filled bubbles floated out of the tube in his lungs. Fifteen minutes later, his heart rate dropped to forty-seven beats a minute and his skin turned ashen.

"Code Blue! Code Blue! Code Blue!" the intercom blared, signaling a life-or-death emergency.

The room filled with people in white, each trying to do something, anything. Doctors massaged his heart.

But it was no use. Chad's heart stopped three days, five hours, and thirteen minutes before his first birthday. Officially, he was pronounced dead at 4:30 A.M. But dead of *what?* No one knew.

At 5:45 A.M., the hospital allowed Sallie and Bruce to see their baby boy. An hour later, a nurse entered Chad's room, gathered his lifeless body, and carried it to the hospital morgue.

At 7 A.M., Nurse Rummel made the rounds on her unit at Immanuel, then called Children's to ask about Chad.

"Chad died during the night," a nurse told her.

About the same time, seven bewildered doctors huddled over a stainless steel table bearing Chad's corpse. All wondered the same thing: What killed him? As the autopsy began, one of them spoke into the microphone in monotones:

"The body is that of a Caucasian male infant measuring 74 cm. in length. The scalp is covered by relatively closely cut, dark blond hair. A shaved region is over the right frontal temporal area where a 1 c., recent, sutured incision is observed. The body is opened with the usual Y-shaped incision. . . ."

For over an hour, the pathologists poked and probed and weighed organs. They found blood in the brain and stomach, but no explanation for the bleeding. They discovered the liver mangled, but no clue as to what had attacked it.

What killed the boy? No one knew. The doctors were as perplexed at the end of the autopsy as they'd been in the beginning.

A persistent ring awakened Duane. It was Sallie and Bruce on the phone, tearfully passing on bad news: Chad was dead.

How could that *be?*

Sandy broke down, hysterical. She sobbed and sobbed. Duane tried calming her: "It must have been the Lord's will. Otherwise, he would have lived."

Sandy sobbed some more.

Finally, she asked Duane how he felt.

"You know," he whispered in a voice heavier than iron wood, "that pack fell out of my nose last night. But my nose isn't bleeding. I just want to get some rest."

From Children's Hospital, Sallie and Bruce drove to the Johnsons', where relatives—Harold and Elaine Betten, Jean and Dave Beard, and Sandy's brothers and sisters and their children —tried to console them. Sandy even invited her

pastor over to help her sister and brother-in-law
with their grief.

In the midst of all the woe for little Chad,
Harold started to worry about Duane and Sherrie. They were sick, too, and it didn't look like
they were getting any better. Sandy told Harold
about the night visit to Glover, and recounted
Glover's medical advice. Harold wasn't buying
it. He badgered Sandy to do something. Why
don't you take your husband and daughter to a
doctor who can *help* them?

Did Harold have any ideas? In fact, he did
and about 10 A.M. he drove Sandy, Duane, and
Sherrie to see his own physician. Sandy
thought the new doctor appeared displeased
with them. Perhaps he felt uncomfortable treating people already under the care of a colleague.

Duane needed help walking into the examining room. And when the doctor attempted to
question him, an enigmatic expression, almost
a simper, crossed Duane's face. Duane said
nothing. Attributing Duane's reaction to un-
cooperativeness, the physician told Sandy her
husband refused to answer questions. Could
she help?

"What are you talking about?" she asked,
raising her voice. "That's not like him."

Just then, blood poured out of Duane's nose
and he slumped to the floor in a coma.

* * *

Once in the Immanuel emergency room, Duane's body sped toward a final shutdown. Bleeding and swelling, his brain dispatched continuous seizure impulses, causing his jaw to clasp tightly and his limbs to shake violently in the hands of the emergency room staff. His heart pumped at 180 beats a minute, almost 3 times the average rate. His blood pressure climbed to 230/120, from an average 120/80.

By noon, Duane wanted to die, but an endo-tracheal tube forced him to suck in air despite the blood clogging his airways. A spinal tap disclosed blood in his entire central nervous system. That came as no surprise: His platelets were down to about 7,000. All of the barriers that kept Duane's blood in its proper channels were breaking down. The patient's entire body was turning into a mere container for his blood.

Duane's condition was so critical, he never made it to intensive care. He went straight from the emergency room to the postintensive care unit on the sixth floor.

Every ten minutes, the staff checked his vital signs: blood pressure, pulse, respiration, pupils, lungs, skin color. No one expected him to improve, yet no one knew what was killing him. Doctors considered surgery, but rejected the idea: The low platelet count could only lead to more bleeding during the operation.

Thursday afternoon, September 14

Early in the afternoon, Nurse Rummel happened to be on the sixth floor talking with Cathy Mabrey, the sixth-floor supervisor.

"We just had the saddest case come in," Mabrey told Rummel. "It's a young man. He's dying and his nephew just died last night."

Mabrey had all of Rummel's attention. "Who was his nephew?"

"I'm not sure of the name," Mabrey said, "but he just died at Children's this morning."

Rummel asked for a description of the uncle's symptoms.

"This is a normal, healthy man who suddenly became acutely ill," Mabrey read from Duane's chart. "He went into a coma and didn't regain consciousness. He was bleeding from everywhere: from his eyes, nose, mouth, anus. His nail beds were blue."

"Oh my God," gasped Rummel, "that sounds like the little boy we transferred."

Mabrey picked up a phone at the nurses' station, dialed Duane's room, and asked the nurse there to find out the name of the nephew from Duane's family.

Chad Shelton.

"Oh my gosh, that's the little baby we had on my floor," said Rummel to Mabrey. "Something very, very bad is going on here. We had normal people and now one is dead and one is dying."

On her way down to the fifth floor, Rummel tried to think of a disease that would affect an infant and cause an adult to die. She drew a blank. Once at her own nurses' station, she called Glover's office.

"Did you know that Chad Shelton and a man named Duane Johnson were relatives?"

"No," responded Glover, surprised. "I wasn't aware of that."

"The uncle is here, very much like Chad. I'm worried about this," Rummel continued. "We had healthy people and now we have one dead and one gravely ill. Maybe we have a contagious disease."

Glover agreed with Rummel, and told her he would immediately consult with two specialists in an effort to find out what was annihilating Duane's insides. Glover called Dr. John R. Feagler, a hematologist or blood expert, and asked him to take a look at Duane. Glover also talked to Dr. John Greene, a neurosurgeon.

Greene soon discovered that Duane's internal bleeding had spread to his brain. Feagler studied Duane's charts and noted that Duane's platelet count was abysmally low.

In Feagler's opinion, a severe lack of platelets in the bloodstream often indicated the platelets were being destroyed by either of two causes: immune mechanisms or nonimmune mechanisms.

Immune mechanisms are body-made substances that attack the platelets; nonimmune destruction of platelets results from a virus, a toxic substance, or blood coagulation in the blood vessels.

The treatment for both problems involved plasmapheresis, in which the patient's blood is removed, and the plasma—the medium the actual cells move around in—is replaced by new plasma. In essence, plasmapheresis is something like a human oil change.

But Immanuel Medical Center lacked the technical capabilities for the cleansing procedure. Preparations were made to transfer Duane to another hospital, Bishop Clarkson Memorial.

In light of Duane's condition, Immanuel doctors asked Sandy to put Sherrie in the hospital, too. Sandy agreed, but emphatically told everyone that under no circumstances would her daughter stay at Immanuel under the care of Glover. Sherrie would go to Clarkson with her father.

By now, small blood spots peppered Sherrie's face. Tests showed she, too, possessed a remarkably low platelet count, only nine thousand, and an enlarged liver. Would blood ooze out of her eyes and mouth as it had with Duane?

"What is this horrible thing that's killing these people?" Rummel thought as Sherrie was being admitted temporarily to Rummel's pediatric unit. "I've never seen this. They're dying so fast we don't even have time to help them."

Was it a contagious disease? Feagler, the hematologist, said he didn't know. But, as a precaution, he ordered Rummel to put Sherrie in "strict isolation."

"We have to be very, very careful here," Rummel told her staff when this was done. "We don't know what we're dealing with."

The message was clear: Don't Take It Home to Your Kids. Everyone took Rummel's advice to heart. Each time anyone entered the girl's room, they donned isolation garb: blue cap, blue face mask, yellow gown, latex gloves, blue booties. On the way out, everything was discarded in a wastebasket and hands were scrubbed with hot water. Throughout the afternoon, the staff even seemed reluctant to walk too near the closed door leading to the girl's room.

Shortly before midnight, an ambulance transported both Johnsons to Clarkson Hospital.

Less serious illnesses demanded compassion, that a father and daughter share a room. Not this one. The staff didn't want Sherrie to think she was in a mortuary with a new arrival.

In room 799, her father lay in bed, motionless: warm, but pale and eyes fixed and bleeding.

Greene had been the neurosurgeon who determined Duane's internal organs were bleeding like ruptured pipes. In his laconic, euphemistically worded report dictated later that evening, he wrote: "The patient, I think, has essentially gone into or approached a neurological situation from which he cannot be retrieved."

Added Feagler, the blood expert:

"The prognosis for this patient is horrible and the wife and family have been so informed."

Doctors also warned Sandy that they gave little Sherrie a diminishing chance for survival.

Friday morning, September 15

The electroencephalogram attached to Duane's brain went flat at 10:25 A.M., a day after Chad had succumbed. At noon, a pathologist studied Duane's corpse to try to unravel the mystery.

He rolled the scalp forward and sawed open the skull. He'd never seen anything like it. It frightened him. Large chunks of the brain were *gone*. The skull was mostly empty, like a cave. Only a few red blood cells swam around, aimlessly.

What had viciously attacked the brain had also ravaged the liver: The pitiful remainder had a nutmeg appearance.

It was obvious the patient had bled to death. But the pathologist didn't have a clue as to why.

Three

THE DEATHS OF Duane and little Chad devastated the Johnsons and Sheltons. One by one family members wandered into Clarkson Hospital. Sandy and her infant son Michael spent the night there—keeping a vigil over Duane and Sherrie. Fifteen minutes after Duane expired, Sandy and Michael were also admitted for observation.

Sallie and Bruce Shelton had recovered, somewhat, from their initial headaches and vomiting bouts, but they were still weak. They, too, were admitted to the hospital. That meant that all five surviving members of both families were now under observation at the Clarkson facility.

Even Harold and Elaine Betten appeared at the emergency room, although it seemed apparent their symptoms were likely psychological.

Still, doctors ordered platelet counts on them, as well.

The flurry of the new patients and blood-curdling rumors from the autopsy room panicked the hospital staff, which ordered every member of the two families placed in isolation. No one was to enter their rooms without "gowning up." Whatever it was, it might be contagious, and if it was communicable it had to be contained.

When Jean and Dave Beard brought a minister to Clarkson to comfort the sick families, they were all hustled into a waiting room and ordered to stay there. Since the Beards and the minister were as baffled and frightened as everyone else, they obeyed. Eventually, the nurses realized they had no authority to quarantine the three indefinitely and allowed them to leave. But that was five hours later. Even then, the nurses treated them like lepers.

Meanwhile, in another part of the hospital, Sherrie Johnson continued to deteriorate: She slept most of the time and when awake, couldn't talk without slurring her words. Worse, her platelet count kept dropping.

Doctor Glover was no longer considered the attending physician to the stricken families; now all the experts were in the game. But the mystery of the illness of the two families continued to perplex Glover.

Glover was forty-seven years old and had started his career as a high school math and science teacher. He hadn't been able to afford medical school, at least not right away. After graduating from high school in his native Broken Bow, a small town in the central part of Nebraska, he enrolled at Kearney State Teachers College. He studied a year, took two years off to work, then returned to the college to graduate in 1955. He taught for several years before obtaining a master's degree, which helped him land a job as a chemistry teacher in Omaha.

By 1963, Glover was married and raising four children. But he had saved enough money and had procured enough student loans to enter the University of Nebraska Medical Center in Omaha. Upon graduating and completing a two-year internship at Immanuel Medical Center, Glover joined the Northwest Clinic in 1968.

Now, after almost ten years as a family practitioner, Nurse Rummel's words reverberated in his mind: "I'm worried about this. We had healthy people and now we have one dead and one gravely ill."

The second one was now dead, too.

Glover had to wonder: What if it was an infectious disease? The outbreak seemed far too big, too serious, for a few doctors or one hospital. Late that Friday afternoon, Glover telephoned the Omaha–Douglas County Health Department to report the strange death of two patients.

John Wiley took the call. As the depart-

ment's epidemiologist—in essence, a disease
detective—he was charged with investigating
food poisonings and unusual health problems.
This one sounded more than unusual, and after
talking with Glover, Wiley hurried down the
hall to notify his boss, Dr. Warren R. Jacobson,
the director of the health department. Jacobson
ordered his epidemiologist to immediately contact all the doctors and hospitals involved for a
meeting.

To Jacobson, the two deaths bordered on
the bizarre. Indeed, they were. It would take
months and dozens of experts to solve one of
the most inscrutable medical mysteries in recent history. The answer, when it was finally
discovered, would be fraught with sinister di-
mensions. Even worse, those who survived
would be left entangled forever in a nightmare
that would have no end.

Four

Saturday, September 16

CHILDREN'S MEMORIAL HOSPITAL—usually a quiet, sleepy place on Saturday mornings—teemed with activity the day after the death of Duane Johnson.

Taking the lead in the epidemiological investigation, health department director Dr. Warren Jacobson convened an emergency meeting there of the city's medical community. He sought answers to two questions:

- What was killing the families?
- Was it contagious?

Over thirty men and women crowded into a small conference room on the first floor of the hospital. They included attending physicians, pediatricians, hematologists, epidemiologists, hospital social workers, medical students, and several staff members of the county health department. They represented some of the city's best medical minds. Some of them brought medical histories, lab reports, and other documents prepared on the patients. Dr. R. David Glover had been invited to attend, but he chose, instead, to see patients at his clinic, even though his two partners were working that morning, too.

Inconspicuous among the many concerned faces at the meeting was Dr. J. P. Lofgren, an epidemiologist with the Centers for Disease Control (CDC) of the U.S. Public Health Service in Atlanta, Georgia. Soon after Glover reported the deaths the previous day, Jacobson requested assistance from CDC, which immediately dispatched Lofgren from Missouri. He was the nearest agent to Nebraska and had to drive all night to be present at the gathering, arriving in Omaha at two in the morning. He took notes quietly during the presentations.

The session began with the primary treatment doctors giving an overview of the patients: the onset of vomiting, headaches, and bleeding. Other physicians described the results of spinal taps, CAT scans, and laboratory tests. Yet others reviewed the exhaustive efforts to arrest the symptoms and what worked and what did not. The critical clues stood out: vomiting, decreased platelets, and liver damage.

Glaringly apparent, too, were the misdiagnoses. Doctors had concluded, at one time or another, that Chad, Duane, and Sherrie suffered from Reye's syndrome. Hogwash! piped one doctor. Other specialists displayed more diplomacy. They pointed out that Reye's syndrome seldom, if ever, caused bleeding, and the disorder did not typically result in massive liver damage.

That morning, the pathologists who did the autopsies on Chad and Duane still couldn't explain why the patients developed such a serious bleeding problem. But they had made a telling discovery: The bodies revealed no evidence of viral infection or a recognizable bacterium. The ghastly deaths, in their opinion, were more consistent with a toxic substance.

A toxic substance? Yes, the pathologists nodded. Probably some kind of food or chemical.

Those in attendance thought they could make little headway until the substance was identified. That was crucial; it might determine the fate of the survivors.

Indeed, the toxic-substance theory sounded the most plausible, especially amid so many medical uncertainties. However, everyone overlooked an essential: The lab tests also failed to identify—or even detect—a toxic substance. Had the pathologists missed the mark? Or was it a bacterium no one had ever heard of? But if so, where was it?

Right or wrong, the group concluded no one needed to be quarantined. The sick should be allowed to mingle with the general hospital population.

Before adjourning the meeting, Jacobson ordered that the Johnson and Shelton homes undergo a thorough search for the killer agent.

Word of the medical conference leaked out to the news media, eager for news of odd and unexplained deaths. Such stories always made the front page or the top of the broadcast—exactly where journalists liked to park their egos. A knot of impatient reporters recognized the long, lean frame of the health director as he prepared to leave the hospital. They rushed at him, shouting out variations of the same questions: Was a contagious disease spreading through the city? Did it have its inception at a recent Septemberfest attended by the families?

No! and No!

The health director needed to be as emphatic as he could. Averting panic was his primary concern, and he didn't want a single reporter misunderstanding his response. After the short answers, he elucidated: Some of the patients, in fact, *had* gone to Septemberfest the previous weekend, but no one else at the festivities turned up ill, indicating the lack of secondary cases. The illness was limited to the extended family. Besides, Jacobson said, a toxic substance, rather than an infectious disease, was believed responsible. The dead and sick inhaled, absorbed, or ingested the toxin.

"We see no threat to the rest of the community," he said with a smile, "including associates of the family."

By late morning, J. P. Lofgren of CDC and John Wiley of the health department stood on the cracked sidewalk facing the Johnson home.

Eerie. Half the house was painted blue, the other half yellow. Several paint cans still sat in the front yard, just as Duane Johnson had left them. Could it be in the paint?

Get rid of it, Sandy Johnson had told her mother. She didn't want to step inside the house again. Too many bad memories. Too many heartaches.

The two epidemiologists were accompanied by an army of inspectors with expertise in plumbing, heating, home construction, health, sanitation, and the environment. None of them knew what they were looking for, but as they fanned out to apply their specialties, they seemed oblivious to any danger.

The sanitation inspector ventured into the neighborhood, searching for anything unusual. At each home, he knocked and asked: Has anyone in your family been sick recently? Have you had any trouble with the sewers? Have you noticed any odors? Do you know of anyone who has been spraying or using chemicals?

A health department employee focused on the gallon paint cans. He wrote down the brand:

Best—The Performer—tulip yellow
#53814 Acrylic Exterior Latex Flat
House Paint.

The environmentalist walked around the property as if on a stroll in the park. He stared down at the grass, then up in the air, then back down at the grass. Reaching two large cottonwoods growing just west of the house, he gazed up at three large squirrel nests hidden in the thick branches. After poking around that side of the house a bit more, he took out a pad and wrote:

"The window air conditioner in the west wall of the home was under one tree and had no air filter. It is likely that these trees are used for roosting by migrating starlings, blackbirds, and grackles. It might be wise to check the soil for the presence of high levels of histoplasma capsulatum, etc."

Histoplasma is a yeastlike fungus disease in soil contaminated by bird feces.

A city inspector examined the rusting window air conditioner, but observed no bacteria buildup. Another inspector checked for cross-connected plumbing lines that might allow sewage to contaminate the drinking water. The plumbing was fine.

Lofgren and Wiley entered the home slowly, taking shallow sniffs to detect any odd smells. The front door opened onto a small area belonging both to the living room, to the left, and the kitchen, to the right.

The two disease detectives gravitated to the kitchen. More signs of life abruptly coming to a tragic stop. On the table lay the remnants of a snack: half-eaten sandwiches and a glass nearly full of an unknown liquid. Lofgren emptied the contents of the glass into a sterile plastic bag for laboratory study, while Wiley collected sugar from a sugar bowl, a package of Kool-Aid lemonade powder, and a sample of Lipton's Instant Tea. A pitcher used to mix beverages was also taken.

The men opened the refrigerator door and took turns sticking their heads in. Nothing piqued their interest.

Next, Lofgren and Wiley checked the cabinets used for storing dishes and breakfast food. They looked, specifically, for signs that the shelves were lined, at one time or another, with insecticide shelf paper. They hadn't been.

One item in a cabinet caught their eye: firecrackers. They contained phosphorus, which could be toxic. The firecrackers were added to the cache of confiscated household articles.

The cabinets under the kitchen sink held the usual array of cleaning agents. None of them applicable.

The men moved on to the bedrooms. They looked in every closet and under every bed.

In Sherrie's room—near a white hamper full of stuffed animals, including a three-foot-tall

yellowish dog with a white snout—the epidemiologists came across a vaporizer. The Johnsons
apparently used it when they believed they suffered from a severe cold or the flu. Water from
the vaporizer was put in a sterile plastic bag.

After several hours of scrutinizing everything, Lofgren and Wiley locked the front door
and left.

From there, they led the search team to the
home of Sallie and Bruce Shelton nearby. The
group followed the same routine and took various water samples after inspecting the kitchen,
bathroom, and bedrooms. It was almost dark
by the time the team left that house.

There was nothing obvious—at either home
—to suggest how several members of the two
families had been toxically contaminated.

Five

AFTER WHAT APPEARED to be a fruitless search of the two homes, J. P. Lofgren spent the rest of the weekend interviewing the families to identify a link—a common experience—between the dead and ill. He wanted to know when they had been together last and what they had consumed. To Lofgren, the patients probably had ingested the toxin, as opposed to breathing it or absorbing it through the skin, since everyone had vomited: the stomach's way of expelling harmful material.

The hospital wasn't the best place to conduct interviews—with doctors, nurses, and technologists scurrying in and out of the rooms —but, at least, those he wished to talk to were in one location. Lofgren introduced himself to all the family members, then methodically asked each of them what they had done on the first day they had vomited and what they had eaten or drunk.

A startling revelation emerged: Lemonade had killed Chad and Duane. More precisely, something in the lemonade made at the Johnson home had poisoned them. As inconceivable as lemonade sounded, it was the most likely vehicle. And judging from the toxin's success, a small amount was very powerful.

As Lofgren pieced together the information supporting his hypothesis, he jotted down his thoughts, to later put in a report for his supervisors at CDC:

"These families had not been together for about a week until the 10th Sept. when the Shelton family came over to the Johnson household for one hour between 3-4 P.M. During this time they sat in the kitchen and living room and Chad Shelton crawled back and forth. Around 3:15 Sandy Johnson poured . . . from a white plastic pitcher with a white cover . . . some lemonade and put some ice in it for this family. Bruce Shelton drank a couple of gulps and gave approximately ¾ of an inch in a nontippable glass to Chad Shelton. Sallie Shelton drank the rest. The Shelton family went on to a birthday party . . . at which there were 15 other people. None of them got sick. On the way home Bruce Shelton and Sallie Shelton started to feel suddenly upset to the stomach and nauseated.

"In the Johnson household, Sandy Johnson did not like lemonade and never drank it even when she made it. She always used the white plastic container with the white top, into which she poured the entire contents of a prepackaged envelope of lemonade, added sugar and water, and stirred with a spoon with a broken handle. She does not recall when she made the lemonade but perhaps as long as three days prior to Sunday, September 10. Susan Conley did not like lemonade but drank it on occasion. Duane Johnson and Sherrie Johnson liked the lemonade very much. Michael Johnson was too small and drank only formula made with boiled water.

"The morning of the 10th, Sandy Johnson had risen with Sherrie Johnson around 10 A.M. and Sherrie Johnson had eaten a small amount of dried cereal with sugar and milk. She may have drunk lemonade as often Sandy Johnson left a glass with either lemonade or water in the refrigerator and Sherrie Johnson would get it on her own . . . Sherrie Johnson vomited around 11 A.M. . . .

"Duane Johnson went up to work on painting the house, but Harold Betten and Elaine Betten came over so Duane Johnson went into the house and was seen to drink 1–2 glasses of an ice-containing liquid, but it is unknown whether it was water or lemonade. Harold Betten and Elaine Betten fixed themselves coffee with boiled water. Harold Betten put sugar into his coffee. Duane Johnson and Harold Betten had a piece of pecan pie and Elaine Betten had a bite. Around noon Duane Johnson had the on-set of vomiting acutely. . . .

"Susan Conley had gotten up at 6 A.M. and had pecan pie and had gone to bed and woke up around noon. Between noon and 3 P.M., Susan Conley tasted some of the lemonade and felt that it tasted bad. She told Sandy Johnson and thought that it had been tossed out prior to the Shelton family coming over. Sandy Johnson did not remember when she tossed out the bad lem-onade but knows that she never made a batch thereafter. The Sheltons are sure they drank lemonade.

"The incubation period of the people in the Shelton family was between 2¾ hours (in the case of Sallie Shelton) and 3 and ¾ hours for Chad Shelton and Bruce Shelton. The incuba-tion period possibly was on the order of 1 hour for Duane Johnson and Sherrie Johnson."

Lofgren reviewed the events leading up to the outbreak on Sunday, September 10. On that day, ten people had been in the Johnson home: five became ill (Sallie, Bruce and Chad Shelton and Duane and Sherrie Johnson) and five did not (Sandy Johnson, Michael Johnson, Susan Conley, Harold Betten, and Elaine Betten). Those who died or got sick drank lemonade made by Sandy for her husband. He liked to drink it year-round.

Toxins were beyond Lofgren's specialty, but he took a moment to think of a substance capa-ble of killing in such a disturbing way. There were some organic materials that often caused liver damage, but most did not disrupt the platelets. Copper sulfate, too, fit the bill, but it damaged the body's intestines and the autopsies disclosed no such injury. When Lofgren gave up toying with the possibilities, he was no closer to identifying the toxin.

Before going to bed at his hotel, Lofgren drew a chart of those afflicted:

PEOPLE VISITING J HOUSEHOLD
SEPTEMBER 10

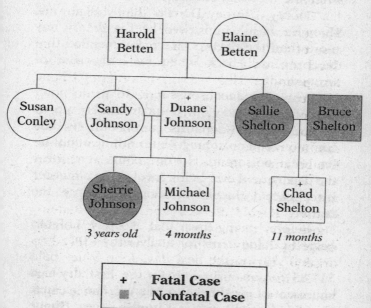

The following day, a Monday, the epidemiologist explained his theory to a second meeting of physicians and health officials. Dramatic as it sounded, his revelation hit a medical black hole: Few individuals realized how it fit, medically. In the eyes of the physicians, Lofgren had presented a square piece of information for a gap they perceived to be round.

But for health director Jacobson, the theory carried a sinister foreboding: It sounded like the members of the two families had been intentionally poisoned. But by whom? And how? After the meeting, Jacobson telephoned Douglas County Attorney Donald "Pinky" Knowles. Knowles wasn't impressed by the theory any more than the doctors. He recommended that Jacobson call back when he had proof of wrongdoing.

What was Jacobson supposed to do now? He and those who worked under him knew a lot about diseases—hepatitis at restaurants and common food poisoning—but nothing about intentional poisoning. No one could remember the department ever being involved in a murder investigation. Jacobson decided to drop the matter.

Before leaving town that Monday, Lofgren helped catalog items for analysis by CDC.

At 7:30 A.M. the next day, John Wiley paid $17.85 for an airline to fly the first dry-iced shipment of specimens to Atlanta. The package contained: eight tissue samples from Duane

Johnson; three sugar samples from a sugar bowl and Tupperware containers; two packages of Kool-Aid mix (unsweetened), pink lemonade flavor and cherry flavor; water samples; an unidentified liquid; and an ice cube tray.

On Wednesday morning, Wiley sent a second package containing: Tupperware; a silver spoon; twenty firecrackers; a bottle of milk or baby formula; liquid from a pan under the kitchen sink of the Johnson home, and urine and blood from Duane, Sandy, and Sherrie Johnson and Sallie and Bruce Shelton.

From then on, the hunt for the mysterious lethal substance would be in the hands of CDC and its crack laboratory sleuths. The task would prove a formidable challenge.

Six

"NATI," HER MOTHER nicknamed her as a child in their native Germany. It was short for Renate, but she rarely shared her nickname with those in her adopted country, the United States. She found Americans couldn't—or wouldn't—pronounce it with an "eh" at the end and her mother's gentle inflection. It wasn't out of arrogance Renate felt so particular about her pet name, for she was not an arrogant woman. She couldn't quite explain it herself, but she knew it had something to do with her childhood: The name simply represented too many special memories for it to be bandied about by just anyone.

Born Renate Dora Albrecht in Hanover, Germany, on January 14, 1933, Renate was only five years old when her father died. His death forced her mother to move to her parents' farm in Godshorn, a town five miles outside Hanover. A couple of years later, her mother's parents passed away, leaving Renate and her mother to run the farm.

Those were the frightening days of World War II, which forever taught Renate the value of life. Dodging bombs became as routine as gathering eggs from the chickens. Sometimes, the air raids lasted days. Wondering whether she played or slept enough seldom occurred to her. There was no time. Survival shaped her every thought. Even as an adult, she'd say: "There are many women who worry about how they dress and how their hair looks. I find that rather nonessential." When the bombing ceased, Renate and her mother returned to farming. Besides keeping food on the table, the cows, pigs, sheep, and horses instilled a work ethic in Renate that would propel her even beyond her father's academic and professional achievements. He had been a researcher with a Ph.D. in physics.

Renate studied English, French, and Latin in elementary and high school, and in her junior year traveled to the United States, graduating from Washington High School in Milwaukee in 1951. Upon returning to her native country, she completed her senior year in the German school system and started a premed program at the University of Göttingen. There, she met Raymond Kimbrough, an American chemistry student on a Fulbright scholarship.

They married in 1956. Two years later, after Renate completed medical school, the Kimbroughs moved to the States.

The next twenty years forged Dr. Renate Kimbrough into a nationally recognized toxicologist. It was by accident she strayed from her love of family medicine and into the world of research and toxins. In her traditional German outlook, her husband's career came first, which meant moving where he moved. Still, she needed to keep her mind sharp and her outlook on life fresh. To do that, she searched out part-time jobs related to medicine.

She obtained her first research job in 1958 in New York at the Memorial Hospital for Cancer and Allied Diseases. Day in and day out, she sifted through thousands of old mildewing medical records to identify diseases associated with cancer. The purpose? Health officials wished to explore the likelihood of a person getting cancer if he or she suffered from a specific disease.

After giving birth to her first child, a daughter, in 1959, she followed her husband to Atlanta, where he accepted a position as an instructor in the chemistry department of the Georgia Institute of Technology. In 1962, the Kimbroughs had a son. Soon after, she applied for a part-time job in the toxicology section of the Centers for Disease Control. Hired as an experimental pathologist, she studied livers to learn the effects of pesticides on people. Her third child, a boy, was born in 1966. About 1968, Kimbrough became an employee of the Federal Drug Administration when the government moved the CDC lab into the FDA's office in Atlanta. In 1970, the lab moved again, this time into the Environmental Protection Agency, making her an EPA employee. A decision to relocate the EPA lab to North Carolina in 1973 prompted Kimbrough to quit. Fortunately, CDC set up another toxicology section in Atlanta. She was back where she'd started a decade before.

By the mid-1970s, Kimbrough had played a key role in solving the mysterious death of horses in riding arenas in Missouri and the Legionnaires' disease outbreak in Pennsylvania. From the beginning, she insisted the Legionnaires' deaths involved a bacterium, not a poison. Her research also made the most prestigious journals: "The Sterilizing, Carcinogenic and Tetatogenic Effects of Metepa in Rats"; "Toxicity of Hexamethylphosphoramide in Rats"; "Spontaneous Malignant Gastric Tumor in a Rhesus Monkey"; "Chlorinated Hydrocarbon Insecticides in Plasma and Milk of Pregnant and Lactating Women."

The excitement of researching rare infectious diseases—and identifying toxins—made her forget about opening her own medical practice.

* * *

It was to Kimbrough's desk that the Omaha specimens were delivered.

Before the physician-researcher opened the packages—which arrived on Wednesday, September 20, and Thursday, September 21—a CDC employee brought out a large ledger and gave the Omaha case a number: 8-26. It had been a busy week. The previous ledger entries included: "5 soil samples from PCB spill in N.C."; "Flour samples from Nigeria"; "Dallas DEA—Mj samples"; and "More human tissue from St. Louis." Without the ledger number, a case could not be accepted by CDC's Toxicology Branch, Clinical Chemistry Division of Bureau of Laboratories.

Although Kimbrough had not traveled to Omaha, she was intimately familiar with details of the epidemiology investigation. She'd been telephonically consulted since Duane Johnson's death. That Friday, a researcher in CDC's Infectious Disease Section contacted her from another CDC building.

"I just got this call from Omaha," epidemiologist Phillip Ladrigan said. "I wanted to let you know about it, just in case."

Ladrigan explained the circumstances of the deaths and informed her that an epidemiologist from Missouri was on his way to Nebraska.

"Do you think this could be a poisoning?" he finally asked.

Kimbrough thought there was an outside

chance and suggested that a variety of tissue samples be taken from Duane. It was too late to do the same with Chad. To find out with any certainty if a toxin had killed the Omahans, she told Ladrigan, she needed to examine tissue under a microscope.

Over the weekend, Ladrigan called Kimbrough at home.

"Omaha is wondering what sort of chemical might cause the illnesses?"

"I don't know," Kimbrough responded impatiently, "but I want to see the tissue. Maybe that will give me some ideas."

Now, Kimbrough had the tissue, J. P. Lofgren's report, the white lemonade pitcher, and the broken spoon used to stir the lemonade. She immediately went to work.

Even though the pitcher had been washed, Kimbrough believed she might be able to extract traces of the toxic substance to identify it. To do so, she mixed a small solution of citric acid and agitated it in the pitcher for several hours. Then she let the blend sit in the pitcher a couple of days.

Disappointingly, the acid extracted no toxins.

Two rats were fed tiny amounts of the solution at two-hour intervals. The rats didn't vomit or bleed.

While those rodents were under observation, Kimbrough injected different rats with solutions containing tap water, unused lemonade, and sugar from the Johnson home. They remained healthy, too.

All the animals were killed several days later, to simulate the patients' survival time before dying. Their livers were normal, even under microscopic examination.

The liver, Kimbrough felt, held the answer to the riddle: It had sustained the most damage. Many man-made and naturally occurring substances affected the liver, but most of them caused damage to many other organs as well. It was unusual to find mostly the liver destroyed. She examined Duane's tissue for arsenic, selenium, and bromide, compounds that specifically attacked the liver. Nothing.

Duane's lungs had bled considerably before death, so she conducted tests for paraquat. Exposure to the weed killer invariably ended in death after ravaging a person's lungs. The tests were negative for the chemical.

What else could it be?

Kimbrough considered the weather in Omaha. Hot and humid. At the time Chad and Duane died, it had been unseasonably hot with 90-percent humidity.

Maybe the killer was aflatoxin, a toxic fungus known to infect peanuts stored improperly in warm and humid regions of the world.

If the weather played any part in the deaths, ergotis, another poisonous fungus, also merited consideration. Contaminated grain brought on the fungus. Even rye meal or rye bread prepared from rye containing the fungus was poisonous. Symptoms included headaches, convulsions, or a coma. Pregnant women made ill by the fungus often aborted their unborn child.

Historically, ergotis was known as St. Anthony's fire or holy fire. As early as the Middle Ages, entire populations suffered from ergotis. In droves, they marched to the shrine of St. Anthony for relief, which came in the form of a diet free of contaminated grain.

Kimbrough didn't completely rule out aflatoxin or St. Anthony's fire, but she tended to discount them: No peanuts or grain were found in the Johnson and Shelton homes and there was no evidence the families shared a common meal before the illnesses.

Not often did Kimbrough find herself unable to make a diagnosis. But she wasn't the only one.

Some of the few tissue samples from Chad had been sent to the Denver Poison Lab in Bionics in Denver, Colorado. The private poison laboratory was a division of Metpath Corporation, a New Jersey–based corporation with clinical and toxicology labs across the nation. Toxicologists there didn't even know where to start.

It was dead end after dead end.

By Monday, September 25, a very frustrated

Kimbrough notified John Wiley of the Omaha–Douglas County Health Department: "I've been unable to identify the toxin. I don't know what to tell you."

Book Two
SOMETHING'S NOT RIGHT

Seven

SOMETHING NAGGED AT LIEUTENANT Foster Burchard, something he'd read in the *Omaha-World Herald*, or *"Weird Herald,"* depending on one's view of the newspaper, the only major metropolitan daily in the country still selling for a dime. Glancing over the front page on Monday morning—as he did every weekday after getting to work at 7:30 A.M.—reminded him of two stories.

One appeared with the headline: DOCTOR: TOXIC MATTER CAUSED ILLNESS. "Toxic" drew his eye. Said the article:

"Although the exact cause of the deaths of two members of an extended family and the illness of several others still isn't known, the rest of Omaha can breathe easier, a health official said Saturday.

"Dr. Warren Jacobson, Omaha–Douglas

County health director, told a press conference at Children's Hospital that autopsies indicate a toxic substance . . . was responsible.

" 'We see no threat to the rest of the community, including associates of the family,' he said."

The second story carried the headline: LEMON DRINK ONE SUSPECT AS CAUSE OF FAMILY ILLNESS. His eyes stopped on "Lemon Drink."

Toxic matter? Lemon drink?

Lieutenant Burchard ran the department's homicide unit. Sudden death was his expertise and his second-generation-cop gut told him something was not right.

The lieutenant inherited both his police instinct and protruding stomach from his father, Foster, a three-hundred-pound bald officer who stood five feet nine. "Baldy," as other uniforms called him, began walking a beat in Omaha in 1906. In those days, cops were required to put in twelve-hour shifts, seven days a week. Once a month, he took a day off from his noon-to-midnight routine.

Lieutenant Burchard would have had far more memories of his father—despite the slavish police workweeks—if Baldy had been younger at the time the lieutenant was born. He was fifty-eight and his wife, Hazel, thirty-seven. In all, the couple raised eleven siblings: four of their own, three from Baldy's first marriage, and four from Hazel's previous one. Baldy died of heart problems on the day his namesake graduated from eighth grade. Yet, Lieutenant Burchard remembered his dad fondly and laughed, loudly, each time he told someone his "old man" walked a beat his entire career because riding in squad cars made him dizzy.

Lieutenant Burchard wasn't quite three hundred pounds, but he resembled his father in most ways: He was short, heavyset, and prematurely balding. The few hairs on his head were gray. By the time he took charge of the homicide unit at the age of forty-five in 1977, he'd put in twenty-one years in the department, including five as the head of internal affairs, a position entrusted only to the most honest cops.

It didn't take long for Lieutenant Burchard's homicide detectives to notice he had almost as little tolerance for sloppy investigative work as he did for crooked cops. They wished he'd slack off a bit when they screwed up, but, overall, they liked working under him: He was fair and favored his mother's levity, a quality badly needed in the world of blood and guts. Those investigators with children most appreciated the lieutenant for attending the autopsies of children, thereby relieving them of the responsibility. Being childless, Lieutenant Burchard was better able to stomach this distasteful job.

Once Lieutenant Burchard finished reading his *Omaha World-Herald*, he leaned back in his chair, lit another thin Benson & Hedges, and waited for Deputy Chief Jack Swanson to come by. Every morning the deputy chief strolled the fourth floor to keep abreast of the major investigations. He stopped at each unit: homicide, vice, robbery-rape, burglary, and fraud. As usual, he paid his brief visit to homicide about 8 A.M.

Lieutenant Burchard and Deputy Chief Swanson were old friends. For years, before age and promotions forced them into sedentary positions, they rode motorcycles together in the traffic unit. Even off duty, they'd ride the back roads of the state.

After discussing their weekends, the lieutenant brought up the Shelton-Johnson case.

"You know, Jack," Lieutenant Burchard said, "I've been following this health department investigation in the *Weird-Herald*. There's something odd about it."

"What's odd about it?" asked the deputy chief, a tall, slender man with black hair slicked back in the 1950s style.

"I'm not sure, but something's not right. The stories keep saying the people died from an illness, but they're looking at a toxic substance."

The deputy chief didn't say anything.

"It doesn't make sense. Do you mind if I check into it? I want to make sure it's not anything we should be interested in."

"Go ahead," came the response. "Just keep me posted."

Mondays were always hectic: Detectives were usually stuck in court helping prosecutors file charges against all those arrested during the

weekend. Lieutenant Burchard put off pursuing
the case until the next day.

Early the following morning, Lieutenant
Burchard telephoned the county health depart-
ment. The receptionist switched his call to John
Wiley.

"Am I glad you called!" Wiley blurted out.

Once again, the lieutenant's sixth sense was
right. That pleased him, but his anger rose the
more he realized the health department suspected foul play and failed to contact the police.

Why the hell didn't anyone call us? he
wanted to yell into the mouthpiece.

Not until much later would he learn of the
health department's attempt to involve the prosecutor. Fortunately that morning, Lieutenant
Burchard opted to question Wiley calmly, instead of castigating him and running the risk of
alienating a critical source of information.

"John, what have you found out? Was it a
disease? An illness?"

"We don't think so," Wiley responded. "We
can't find any disease and neither can the CDC.
We think it's a toxin."

Lieutenant Burchard carefully inched on:
"Do you think they got poisoned accidentally or
do you think somebody poisoned them?"

"It's a possibility."

"Which one?"

"It's possible someone poisoned them."

Lieutenant Burchard could hardly contain

himself: Two persons were dead and no one
considered calling the homicide unit! What the
hell was going on? Who said you couldn't get
away with murder?

"John," the lieutenant said firmly, "if you
don't mind, I'm going to have one of my guys
come out and talk to you."

By 8:30 A.M. three imposing homicide investigators—Sergeant Charlie Parker, Detective
K. G. Miller, and Detective Clyde Nutsch—were
sitting in Wiley's office.

The epidemiologist began his briefing from
the beginning, giving the men the victims'
names, ages, addresses, and their relationship.
He recounted the Sheltons' visit to the Johnson
residence on September 10, listed the common
symptoms, and described the search of the
homes. Then he handed the attentive investigators a written report of the September 16 meeting at Children's Hospital. The report illustrated
how bewildered the medical community had
been at the height of the illnesses.

There were loose ends in the epidemiological investigation, explained Wiley, but there was
no doubt the victims died from drinking lemonade "contaminated with a toxic agent." With
that, he shrugged his shoulders in defeat. The
inquiry had hit a wall.

By the time the meeting ended an hour
later, everyone agreed the Omaha Police Department would enter the case. After the cops
left, Wiley's relief at handing over the reins of

the investigation was noticeable as he slumped in his chair staring at his coffee cup.

On returning to headquarters, the investigators informed their boss someone conceivably had poisoned the victims with spiked lemonade. The potential for murder was very real, but the detectives had trouble fathoming the scenario. It seemed preposterous that anyone could poison an entire family, including children. Unbelievable! Nevertheless, the department now faced that very possibility. Lieutenant Burchard assembled his men in a small room adjacent to his office for a brainstorming session.

Criminal poisonings rarely came along, and they were never easy to solve, if they were ever solvable. Even cyanide poisonings—which killed within thirty to sixty seconds by inactivating the mechanisms that allow cells to use oxygen—were extremely challenging. That elite poison leaves a bitter almond smell lingering in the victims, but few people are capable of recognizing the scent. And, after all, who was to say the victim didn't die from eating apple or cherry seeds, which release cyanide on digestion.

Poisons were everywhere, in varied forms. They infested households: in cleaners, vanity products, and gardening chemicals. Even some plants—the roots of the iris, the berries of the lily of the valley, the leaves of the rhubarb— killed. The selection was endless if a person took the time to do the research. That's what made this particular breed of criminal so dangerous: planning born out of cooled passion.

Criminal poisonings represented one of the most cowardly acts of murder, in Lieutenant Burchard's opinion, since the killer lacked the fortitude to face the victim, opting for slithering through the grass like a snake. And only a slimy snake, he thought, could kill a defenseless child.

In the homicide think tank, the group listed, on a large blackboard, the questions they most needed to answer: Was it accidental or intentional? If it wasn't an accident, who were the likely suspects?

The most important, but elusive, question appeared to be: What killed Chad Shelton and Duane Johnson? Police well understood, as their epidemiological counterparts had, that identifying the poison could help treat the surviving victims. It would also be the best lead in helping identify the poisoner, if there was one.

Already, the chances of solving the case were against police. Even "smoking-gun" murders turned into investigative nightmares if the scene wasn't processed within twenty-four hours of the slaying.

The Shelton-Johnson investigation reeked of its own special problems: The pitcher suspected of containing the poison had been washed and the scene of the crime had been contaminated by the health department search.

Additionally, the killer—if it was murder—did not employ a traditional weapon, denying police the use of such reliable tools as ballistics or blood-splatter patterns. Investigators were definitely out of their comfort zone.

The Shelton-Johnson case suffered from one other drawback, a major one in Lieutenant Burchard's opinion: Ordinary pathologists had done the autopsies. They knew a lot about medicine, but little about crime. For murder victims, the lieutenant demanded forensic pathologists trained in the criminal interpretation of trauma. What did a hospital pathologist know about postmortem wounds? Lividity? Rigidity? Entrance and exit wounds? Or whether a killer strangled the victim manually or with a ligature?

Head injuries were a specific case in point: A blow to the head by an assailant caused a different type of injury to the brain from one caused by a person striking an object in a fall. Forensic doctors could differentiate between such subtle distinctions. They also could detect changes in the brain brought about by life-support systems.

Later in the investigation, it would again infuriate Lieutenant Burchard to learn that the pathologists in the Shelton-Johnson deaths failed to preserve enough tissue for testing.

At the conclusion of the brainstorming session in the think tank, the lieutenant selected one investigator, Detective K. G. Miller, to do the initial spadework. If the workload piled up, others would be assigned to help with select tasks.

Eight

DETECTIVE KENNETH G. MILLER was known as much for his temper as his tenacity. The gray metal filing cabinets containing the murder files served as his personal punching bags. Every time something went awry, he punched them, slapped them, kicked them. He'd get especially angry at them if he couldn't locate a report. On those occasions, he even tried tearing their handles off. If the cabinets were made of flesh and blood, they would have been as black-and-blue, as maimed and mangled, as the victims in the files.

Detective Miller displayed his maddening frustration in public, too. Everyone in the department claimed to have a "Miller temper vignette." If they really didn't, they made one up. What was the difference?

Many of Detective Miller's public blowups had occurred while working as a motorcycle traffic cop with Lieutenant Burchard and Deputy Chief Swanson. Once, while directing traffic at an intersection, he ripped off his helmet and threw it against the windshield of another officer's patrol car because he couldn't get a woman to turn in the right direction. In another instance, an old lady flagged down Lieutenant Burchard in West Omaha to make him aware that some crazy motorcycle officer was "beating" his motorcycle in the middle of a busy intersection. It was K.G., mad about his cycle skidding on the gravel and dumping him.

His wife, Norma, knew exactly why her husband lost his temper: It was inherited. Detective Miller's father and grandfather habitually had exploded with saliva-spitting rage. In fact, his grandfather's outbursts had earned him an involuntary commitment to an institution, mostly for his own protection.

Needless to say, in the good-guy bad-guy routine, Detective Miller seldom played the good guy.

When not thumping the murder files, Detective Miller often hunched his large, stoop-shouldered body over his small desk, one of many occupied by detectives in an open area on the fourth floor. The gray-haired investigator appeared fast asleep—like an old mare in some faraway cornfield—but he wasn't. Occasionally, a colleague tried sneaking up on him to find out what he was doing. Invariably, Detective Miller's head tilted in the direction of the motion. Attempts to tease the detective were few since he also worked on the bomb squad, giving him access to a variety of ways to get even. For those violators who smoked, a favorite was black powder mixed in their ashtray ashes. When the unsuspecting snoop placed his cigarette in the tray, the powder ignited, causing a startling flash and a cloud of smoke. If the offender didn't get the message the first time, Detective Miller was known to add a mixture potent enough to rock the entire desk.

More often than not, he studied small gadgets on his desk. Little things, and how they worked, fascinated the big man. They helped him think. He'd take them apart, then put them together again. He surrounded himself with gadgets. In a suit pocket, he carried a set of folding scissors, a diamond-tip scriber to write on glass, a pocketknife, and a tiny measuring tape. At home, he filled the kitchen drawers with gizmos. He loved to cook, and officers begged to attend poker games at his home. K.G. served delicious canned peppers—his favorites were banana peppers—with homemade Italian sausage.

Temper and oddities aside, the forty-three-year-old native Omahan was one of the department's best homicide investigators. He was meticulous at gathering evidence at crime scenes and sifting through people's pasts. His personal and professional philosophies were simple: Men should wear short hair and look like men and crooks should go to jail. When a criminal would beat the rap against him, Detective Miller, the proverbial man of few words, shook his head from side to side: "That's not right."

By the time Detective Miller started nosing around—just over two weeks after the inception of the outbreak—the mysterious syndrome dissipated enough for the hospital to release all the victims. Sallie and Bruce Shelton and Sherrie Johnson were far from well, but there wasn't much else doctors could do for them.

Sallie survived—with the help of several platelet transfusions—but her mind and body stalled often. The medication she took home did little for her headaches, nausea, and dazed state. Cloudy thoughts, self-deprecation, swirled in her mind. Somehow, she blamed herself for her son's death. In her mind, it was all her fault. On several occasions she told her mother, Jean:

"Mom, maybe I kept Chad too clean. Every time he'd get a spot of dirt playing outside, I'd hurry and clean him up. Maybe I was too good of a mother to him and the Lord took him away from me."

"It wasn't your fault," Jean would say.

Nothing alleviated the heartache over Chad. Sallie vaguely recollected being allowed to leave the hospital long enough to bury him. She saw him, repeatedly, in his tiny casket with a bathtub windup, paddle-wheeled toy boat on the inside of his left arm. It was his favorite toy. His Grandma Jean had given it to him.

Bruce spent only a few days in the hospital, but his headaches never really went away. Both he and his wife suffered permanent liver damage, requiring them to regularly see a doctor as outpatients. With every ache and pain, they worried the original symptoms, in their entirety, would return.

Of the three surviving victims, Sherrie was the luckiest to be alive. She had had one foot in the grave when Dr. Feagler ordered her transferred to Children's Hospital, where he performed the procedure he had hoped to do on her father. Her blood was totally replaced two-and-a-half times before her platelet count improved. Like her aunt and uncle, she was discharged with permanent liver damage, also necessitating outpatient treatment.

Sallie was the last to leave Clarkson Hospital, checking out the day Detective Miller was assigned the Shelton-Johnson case. Unable to reach Sallie or Sandy by phone after lunch, Detective Miller drove to their mother's home.

Jean and her second husband worked as resident-managers of an apartment house on South 29th Street in South Omaha, the heart of the city's ethnic neighborhoods. Most of the homes in the area were owned by Scandinavians, Bohemians, Lithuanians, Germans, Italians, Poles, and Croatians. The Europeans began migrating to the Midwest by the thousands after the railroad helped turn Omaha into a meat-processing mecca in territorial days. Even into the 1950s and 1960s, many of them still labored in the meat-processing businesses adjacent to the smelly—but very profitable—stockyards on L Street in south Omaha.

Jean and Dave had met a decade earlier. The two came from opposite walks of life: She was a city girl, he a homebody rural boy.

Born in Omaha in 1933, Jean was one of eight girls and two boys raised by Alva and Leola Davis, two individuals made for each other in every way, including stature. He stood five feet, she five feet two. Jean would grow no taller than her father.

Throughout their marriage, the Davises were as short on cash as they were on height. And poverty, in their case, meant an existence just shy of rummaging through trash cans for something to eat. Alva kept food on the table and shoes on the kids' feet by delivering coal to various neighborhoods.

Like her mother, Jean attended North High School in north Omaha. And like her mother, she failed to finish high school. After her freshman year, Jean obtained a job packing nail files for a brush company. Being able to afford a few personal amenities meant much more to the impoverished girl than returning to school.

Not long after dropping out, Jean met a youngster named Harold Betten, who preferred people to call him by his middle name, Robert. They married on October 8, 1949. She'd just turned sixteen, he seventeen. Wisely, Mr. and Mrs. Betten chose to wait before having children. Their first arrived in 1951. That was Dan. Then came Sandy in 1952; Ronald in 1954; Sallie in 1957; Susan in 1959; Roger in 1961; Laurie in 1962; and Robert in 1968.

When it came to the children's height, Jean's chromosomes dominated. Family outings conjured up images of elementary students on school field trips.

For the girls, being small offered more advantages than disadvantages. All stood five feet or five feet one, allowing them to wear the same clothes and shoes. Their bodies were so compact that even as adults they wore size five petite dresses and size six shoes, attire often intended for big girls, rather than young mature women.

The Bettens' marriage thrived until the late 1960s, when the union fell apart for reasons that no one could explain. It just happened, as it tragically happened thousands of times a year around the country. Suddenly, decades-old relationships withered inexplicably. Poof, the magic was gone. Where did it go? No one knew.

The crumbling marriage compelled Jean to reenter the work force. She obtained a job making theater stage curtains for schools and auditoriums. Sometimes, instead of hurrying home from work, she dropped by a neighborhood bar for a drink, forcing Sandy, the oldest of the girls, to play mother.

It was there that Jean met John Beard, who also favored using his middle name, Dave, as a first name. He was a big green-eyed man partial to crew cuts and Big Mac overalls. Both enjoyed the boisterous camaraderie of bar life, but it was their love of pool that brought them closest together. As if to cement their relationship, each purchased their own pool cue.

Dave had searched out Omaha in 1958, after tiring of alfalfa, hogs, corn, cows, and anything else that grew or moved in McCook, Nebraska, in the southwest part of the state. The forty-two-year-old fondly remembered growing up on his father's farm—just as many Nebraskans recalled their own childhood experiences in small towns with names like Bloomfield, Ponca, North Platte, Scottsbluff—but he longed to smell something other than farm animals and dry earth.

When he met Jean in 1969, he was working at a filling station during the week and mixing dough at a bakery on weekends. From the start, Dave felt a personal obligation to raise Jean's kids. To bring in extra cash, he started "junking." As soon as he finished mixing dough on Saturdays and Sunday, he hung out at police auctions buying confiscated cars—some that ran and some that didn't—which he sold piecemeal at a profit. Once the children moved in with the Beards, life, for the most part, revolved around card games and listening to records.

Eventually, Dave buckled under the weight of three jobs. He hardly slept. Emphasizing his mechanical skills, he obtained work fixing sewing machines used to close feed bags. The job paid well, but required traveling around the state, leaving little time for the kids. After a year or so, the Beards thought of the perfect solution to most of their problems: apartment managing. Husband-and-wife teams lived in an apartment complex while still drawing a salary. Occasionally, Dave bitched about tenants who wouldn't do anything for themselves, but, generally, the couple enjoyed it and finally made a decent living.

Detective Miller's presence at their front door baffled Jean and Dave Beard. What did the illnesses have to do with the police? Was there something they didn't know about?

Since a toxic substance had killed Chad and Duane, explained the investigator, the police wished to eliminate any chance of foul play. Did the Beards have a moment?

Of course, they said.

When Detective Miller started posing questions, the Beards offered what they presumed to be the most relevant answers: their activities the night before everyone became ill.

"Sandy and Duane went out to see a drive-in movie that Saturday night," Jean began, "but they didn't like it. They left and came over here and we played canasta all night."

"What time did they leave?" asked the detective.

"Not until two in the morning," she said. "Duane had a cold and wasn't feeling well. He wanted to go home, but Sandy wanted to keep playing."

" 'Just one more game,' " Dave quoted Sandy as saying. " 'Just one more game.' "

Susan Conley was at the Beard residence and on hearing the conversation, she joined the interview. Susan did not think much of Dr. Glover. She warned people: "I don't let him take care of Jeff at all."

After explaining why she had been living with her sister, Susan stated that she did not accompany Sandy and Duane to the drive-in but did go out, getting home at 3 A.M.

"Was the house locked when you got home?" inquired Detective Miller.

"Yes," Susan said, "I let myself in with a key."

In familiarizing himself with the health department investigation, Detective Miller noticed a discrepancy regarding when the suspected lemonade was thrown out.

Susan repeated her account. She awoke thirsty about 6 A.M. and took a sip of lemonade. It tasted funny. She was positive she informed her sister of the "bad taste" before the Sheltons dropped by in the afternoon.

Detective Miller pushed into more sensitive ground. How were Sandy and Duane getting along?

There were disagreements, as in any marriage—Susan and Jean bobbed their heads in accord—but no animosity existed between them.

"Who would want to hurt the family?"

The Beards couldn't fathom this new idea of the deaths being murder, let alone think of anyone who could kill in such a way. However, they supplied the visitor with a couple of names, one an old boyfriend and one an ex-husband.

From South Omaha, Detective Miller drove his unmarked car north beyond the city limits to the home of Duane Johnson's parents. They lived near McKinley Street, on a five-acre plot, where they raised a few head of cattle. The Beards told Detective Miller he could find Sallie and Bruce Shelton and Sandy Johnson there.

Sallie and Bruce were stunned at the prospect of someone intentionally killing their son. Murder had never crossed their minds.

Once Detective Miller was able to get the Sheltons and Sandy to confirm the chronology of events in Lofgren's report and to respond to comments made by the Beards, he focused on the lemonade.

Did Sandy discard the lemonade before the Sheltons arrived or not?

Sandy scowled defensively. Her strong reaction surprised Detective Miller. Sandy said she thought little of her sister's comment because Susan was nine months pregnant and complained of everything tasting bad. Sandy assured the investigator she did not throw the lemonade away.

As to the night before the outbreak, Sandy added few details to the account provided by Jean and Dave Beard.

"Did anyone enter the house while you were gone?"

"I don't think so," Sandy answered. "Both doors were locked . . . they have deadbolt locks. Nothing was out of place."

"Is there any other way someone could have gotten in?"

The question reminded her of a bedroom window at the rear of the house. It had no lock and the outside screen came off easily. On at least one occasion, Duane climbed into the house through the window when the family locked itself out.

"Have you seen any prowlers or window peepers?"

"No," she said.

He brought up old boyfriends.

Sandy acknowledged dating a couple of bad apples—and making the mistake of marrying one of them—but she hadn't seen them in years.

How about the one you didn't marry?

He was actually a very nice guy, she said. Peaceful.

Finally, the investigator asked if the victims

believed the lemonade linked the deaths and illnesses. The Sheltons and Sandy could think of no other common denominator.

Detective Miller closed his pocket-sized notebook, thanked the families for their time, and left to return to headquarters in downtown Omaha.

In his estimation, the interviews that day produced few obvious leads. Usually, he was mired in suspects. This time, he had the names of one measly boyfriend and one ex-husband. So far, the deaths didn't strike him as the average boyfriend-girlfriend beef. Commonly in those, hysterical screams startled the neighborhood before the girl staggered outside with an ice pick deep in her chest. When the tables were turned and the woman was the perpetrator, the slug from a .357 Magnum ensured that the bum never woke up from a nap.

The Shelton-Johnson case hinged on more complicated components. Detective Miller weighed some of the possibilities:

An unusual disease wasn't totally out of the equation, he thought. Doctors weren't always right. If they were, the courts wouldn't be clogged with medical malpractice lawsuits. They blamed a toxic substance, yet they couldn't identify it.

Accidental? That was possible, too. All the victims saw the same doctor: R. David Glover. He could have prescribed the wrong medication or the wrong dosage.

The detective's cynical side interjected and he started speculating. Maybe Glover intentionally slipped his patients a toxic substance to focus attention on his lifesaving efforts. Sometimes, firefighters set fires to put them out. It made them heroes. The more Detective Miller thought about the scenario, the less he liked it. Despite all his good intentions, Glover had done little to help the victims. In the medical field, the hero syndrome more aptly applied to nurses, who craved attention.

Back at headquarters, Detective Miller slipped his suit coat off and draped it over the back of the chair at his desk in the detective bull pen. Then he walked to a computer terminal, on the way passing a life-size black crow perched on a dark brown log.

The crow served to remind detectives to be open-minded. Too often, an investigator jumped to conclusions and locked on a suspect in the first days of the investigation. Meanwhile, the real killer left town or bought enough time to cover his tracks. To discourage such tunnel vision, the homicide unit created the Crow Award. Every year in front of the entire detective division Lieutenant Foster Burchard bestowed the award on the homicide detective who picked the wrong suspect in that year's biggest murder case. Usually, several investigators chose the wrong individual, but the award deservedly went to the one who made the biggest

Above and below: Some of the demon cutouts sent by Steven Harper to Sandy Johnson at the home of Jean and David Beard. The S.B. stands for Sandy Betten; her maiden name was Betten and first married name was Murphy.

Above: Rat cages litter a detached garage at Steven Ray Harper's home. Steven used the rats to experiment with toxins.

Below: After his arrest in Beaumont, Texas, Steven Harper used his blood to write SANDY on the jail wall.

Steven Ray Harper in his senior high school picture.

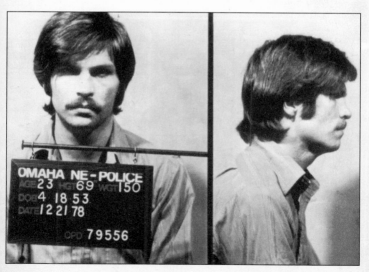

Steven Ray Harper being booked in Omaha after his
extradition from Texas in December 1978.

Above: Douglas County Deputy Prosecutor
Sam Cooper.

Below: East Omahans Jesse and Eva Lou Harper in 1954
after their new home burned to the ground. In Jesse's
arms is their one-year-old son, Steven Ray Harper.

spectacle of himself trying to convince colleagues he was right. At least once, Detective Miller had been the recipient of the Crow Award, and that dubious distinction crossed his mind as he sat down at the computer to examine the players in the poisoning.

It was habit with Detective Miller to run the names of everyone involved in a case through the crime computer, which contained short profiles of individuals arrested on felonies. At the very least, a "hit" provided a person's address and something about their propensities. Some stole, others molested children. On this day, Detective Miller specifically was looking for anyone with violent behavior.

One at a time, Detective Miller typed in the names of the extended family. There were a few traffic tickets here and there, but nothing earth shattering.

The investigator was about to enter the names of Sandy's former boyfriends when the antiquated computer screen blinked and faded to black. It seemed the computer was always malfunctioning. It especially crashed when too many detectives tried using the system at the same time. For some time, the city's purchasing department had talked of replacing the department's electric typewriters with something called word processors—the so-called typewriters of the future—but no one in the entire police department favored the move. Not if they were going to fizz out as often as the crime computer.

Detective Miller leaned forward in his chair to smack the computer terminal to the floor. Maybe that would make it come alive.

"Don't you dare," Lieutenant Burchard shouted from his office. "I'm serious. It'll come out of your paycheck and I'll have you typing everybody's reports for a year."

Detective Miller didn't turn to look at his commanding officer, but he decided to wait for the system to come back up. Once it did a short time later, he typed in the two remaining names. Nothing.

Before going home, Detective Miller made plans to search the Johnson home, the apparent scene of the crime.

The next day, another army of men piled out of several cars at the half-painted shoe box house on Fontennelle Boulevard. This time, the searching eyes sought sinister clues.

Several detectives fanned out to canvass the neighborhood for leads on any suspicious characters. They paid particular attention to the Belvedere Club, located just west of the Johnson home. The club regularly hosted bingo games that attracted people from all over the city. Had a patron strayed to the Johnson home? Employees told police they never noticed anyone paying any special attention to the small rambler. As the plainclothes officers walked away, one employee suggested they touch base with an Omaha uniformed cop who worked security at the club on his off-duty hours.

A young criminalistics technician named Don Veys, who happened to be the mayor's son, snapped photographs of the outside of the house before moving inside to diagram the rooms. Then he dusted for fingerprints: the refrigerator, the doors, living room table, dresser drawers, toilet. He lifted fingerprints from almost every surface, but all were too old or smudged.

Detective Miller donned off-white coveralls over his dress shirt and slacks and concentrated on the doors and wood-framed windows, easily finding the rear one that was hard to secure, as Sandy had said. He spied a heel mark on the siding just below the window and called Veys over to photograph it.

He had hoped to find a footprint, if an intruder had entered through the window. In a case some years back, he had come across a print and he had solved the slaying after trudging to virtually every shoe store in the city in the dead of winter.

On the frame of the Johnson window, the detective also found a single burnt match.

"Had the killer lit it to illuminate his way to the window?" Detective Miller wondered. "Or was it Duane Johnson's match? He smoked."

A wooded area behind the house looked like the perfect place to discard evidence.

"Did the poisoner toss the container with remnants of the toxin into the overgrown grass?"

Detective Miller got on his hands and knees to comb through the grass and debris, with negative results.

Some cases were like that, void of evidence. A very disappointing outing.

Nine

DETECTIVE K. G. MILLER slowed his unmarked car to get a good look at the small house on Fontenelle Boulevard. As he expected, it was vacant. He'd heard Sandy Johnson had refused to return, but he needed to be sure before parking his car to begin shadowing her.

The investigator moved on to the home of Bruce and Sallie Shelton, where he located the Johnson car. About a block away, he intentionally parked with his front end pointing away from the house. The car attracted less attention that way. He could see the house through the rearview mirror.

There, he settled down in street clothes with binoculars, a thermos of hot coffee, Italian sausage sandwiches, and a deck of cards. It had been a while since he'd invited friends to his home for cards and beer. He missed the cops who came for the cards, but he missed more cooking for the guys, who simply enjoyed his culinary creativity.

Lacking any clear direction in the case, the investigator had decided to let his many years of homicide experience dictate his next move. In police work, the unnatural death of a husband or wife made the spouse the primary suspect. And more often than not, the spouse ended up being the perpetrator. Detective Miller had seen it over and over again. In this case, Sandy had even made the lemonade that killed her husband. Had Sandy and Duane been getting along? Had the infamous love triangle claimed more victims? If Sandy was a murderer, where did she get the poison? And what was it? No matter what the motive, the investigator thought, Sandy must have been very unhappy or hated her husband very much to kill him.

Off and on, he tailed Sandy: sometimes during the day, sometimes at night. Even from a distance, she didn't strike him as a woman in mourning. She seemed to him to smile a lot and rarely stay home. At all hours, she'd pack the kids in the car and drive, occasionally with curlers still in her hair. He followed her nearly everywhere: to the home of her mother, to the residence of her real father, to the apartment of a friend. At each stop, he took down the address and license number of the vehicles at the residence. He even tailed her to the supermarket. After she paid and left the store, he flashed his badge at the cash register clerk and asked what she'd purchased. Lemonade? Unusual medication from the pharmacy? A little-known herb? Fresh in his mind was an article he'd read about ethnic herbal remedies, many of which were made from plant chemicals that were toxic.

Winding through the city, trying to keep up with the seemingly atypical widow, the detective couldn't help thinking of past Omaha slayings. The street signs reminded him of them. The urban metal tombstones forever would serve as markers to the moment he'd arrived in the middle of the night to piece together a person's final dreadful hours. Most of the tombstones rattled in the wind on 24th Street in north Omaha, home of many of the impoverished in the city. Those were the easiest murders to solve, for they spawned from impetuous knifings and shootings over drugs or sex. Abundant was the evidence: a knife handle covered with fingerprints, a blood trail to the suspect's house, a roomful of eyewitnesses.

Detective Miller was willing to give almost anything for a single good clue in this case.

After several days of following Sandy with little to show for it, Detective Miller returned to his office. She'd kept no assignation with a lover and she'd led him to no secret stash of potent poison.

But the investigator wasn't so easily satisfied. Besides, something troubled him about Sandy: the intensity of her scowl.

By phone, the detective contacted some of her friends to talk confidentially. He did the same with a number of her teachers. Sandy had attended North High School, like her mother and grandmother. And like her mother and grandmother, Sandy had dropped out. She'd left after her junior year.

While gathering every scrap of information he could about Sandy, Detective Miller received a phone call from the deacon for the fundamentalist church where Sandy and Duane Johnson had worshiped. To help the widow with incidentals, several Omaha churches had organized fund drives. Before releasing any money, however, the deacon sorely needed to know "if there had been any hanky-panky going on."

Detective Miller covered the phone's mouthpiece so the deacon couldn't hear him laugh. Hanky-panky? Did he mean screwing around? Detective Miller finally blurted out: "No, not that I know of."

Somehow, Sandy had found out about the detective snooping around. One of her friends probably had clued her in. When Sandy called the police to complain, Detective Miller lost his temper and inadvertently revealed that he wasn't the only one suspicious of her. Her deacon—of all people—felt it necessary to question her fidelity. Sandy hung up.

The next day, the deacon contacted the investigator. Timidly, he divulged that Sandy had given him an old-fashioned tongue-lashing.

In Detective Miller's words: "She chewed his ass from one end to the other. She even quoted the Bible to him. She got nasty."

The episode soured the detective on Sandy and led him to believe she could not be the born-again Christian she professed to be. But the incident only reinforced what he'd been hearing lately from those who knew her.

Sandy was starting to come into focus, and what Detective Miller saw clashed with a photograph he'd seen of the Johnsons.

Just days before the mysterious deaths, the Johnsons had kept an appointment at a photo studio for a family portrait in front of an elm tree mural. Little Sherrie sat in front of her handsome father, who wore wire-rimmed glasses and a bashful smile. Sandy cradled Michael in one arm. With her broad smile, round blue eyes, and wavy, blond hair, Sandy conveyed the image of the all-American girl.

Developed after the deaths, the photograph did not reflect either Duane or Sandy. Duane was dead and Sandy was far from the soft-spoken girl who sought the quiet life.

It appeared now to Detective Miller that her attractive face and small frame concealed a wild temper and belligerent manner that seemed to manifest itself around men. She craved men, especially those with potential. She seemed to love to mesmerize them. Yet, since puberty, she seemed driven to dominate them.

The result: relationships mutilated by acrimonious fights.

A person simply had to look at her first marriage and a subsequent courtship to realize how hard she rode her men.

Had she been even harsher on Duane Johnson? the investigator wondered.

Seventeen-year-old Jim Murphy became the first boy to feel Sandy's anger. The son of a longtime switchman for the railroad, Jim attended Rummel High School, an all-boys school in Omaha. He met Sandy his junior year in the fall of 1968 while at a Saturday night dance at Notre Dame Academy, an all-girls school.

During the evening, a friend pulled him across the dance floor to introduce him to a slim, well-dressed girl with a hairstyle similar to Marlo Thomas's in the television program *That Girl*. It was Sandy.

"I've always been partial to blondes, but I fell in love with her blue eyes," Jim recalled years later. "She was extremely shy. She'd talk without looking at you. She looked down at the table."

Between songs, Jim flirted with the young lady and found out his new infatuation was a sophomore at North High School. He also learned she had recently broken up with a North High guy named David. Good, thought Jim, she was available. The dance ended at 11

P.M., with Jim and Sandy going their separate ways.

In the following days, Jim telephoned friends to obtain Sandy's phone number. When he finally succeeded, he called her to ask if she could attend the next Academy dance. Sandy agreed, and it wasn't long before they were meeting regularly at dances. Within a few months, Jim was stopping by her house several times a week.

Watching her wash and cook for her father, brothers, and sisters on the nights Jean came home late made Jim want to rescue Sandy. He pitied her, and envisioned himself her knight in shining armor. One day, he'd ride up to the house and carry her away to his castle. For the time being, the teenagers made do making love in the car in remote places.

By 1969, Jim believed Sandy was his girl. He thought they were going steady. But somehow her old boyfriend, David, kept coming into the picture. Jim learned of Sandy's dates with David from overhearing the Betten children talk. In fact, some of them openly told him David was going to beat up Jim for messing with *his* girl. Whose girl was she?

Years later, Jim realized he should have made a bigger issue of the old boyfriend—"put his foot down"—but he didn't because he was "young and dumb." As a result, their courtship tended to be murky.

Sandy's father, Harold, didn't mind Jim

showing interest in this daughter, but Jim's parents did, particularly his dad, Ed. Sandy wasn't good enough for his son, who already was showing a nose for business. Besides, there was nothing "positive" in his son dating a girl whose parents were in the midst of breaking up.

Ed tried discouraging the affair. When Sandy telephoned their home, he'd hang up or say, "He doesn't want to talk to you! He doesn't want to see you anymore!"

Next time she saw Jim, Sandy confronted him: "Your father thinks I'm trash, doesn't he?"

For a moment, Jim bowed his head dejectedly. Then he said: "It's what I think that counts. I love you."

Trying to persuade his son to look for someone else, Ed forbade Jim from escorting Sandy to his senior prom. That infuriated Jim, but he was afraid to disobey his father. Jim told Sandy he wasn't going to the prom. But he did, alone.

Of course, Sandy found out and made him feel like a heel: "You went to the prom? Without me? You lied to your girl? How could you do that?"

Ashamed, Jim vowed to make it up to her.

Ed tried threats when the dating continued: "I'm going to break every bone in your body if you don't stop seeing her!"

"Go ahead . . . if you're big enough," Jim yelled, knowing full well his father would have no problem with a teenager who hardly weighed one hundred pounds.

These bitter confrontations over Sandy would ruin their relationship for life.

Sandy gave her boyfriend hell on the other end: "Why are you letting your parents run your life?"

Jim loved Sandy and asked her to marry him once he graduated from high school in 1970. Sandy was only seventeen and still in school, but she couldn't pass up the opportunity to escape domestic servitude—cooking, cleaning, washing—not realizing she would simply be trading one house for another.

Sandy contacted Jean, who had gone to live with her husband-to-be, Dave Beard. Since she was too young to marry under Nebraska law, Sandy asked for help in tying the knot. Dave Beard made a few phone calls and on June 22, 1970, he and Jean drove the kids nearly two hundred miles to Mankato, Kansas, to be married.

In order to elope, Jim told his parents he was going camping that weekend with some of his friends from school. During the weekend, however, one of the teenagers Jim was supposed to be camping with called the Murphy home. That blew the cover story.

"Shit hit the fan," Jim recalled.

For over two hours, his father yelled and cursed at his son like a marine drill instructor. How could he do this to the family? How could he do such a boneheaded stupid thing? And of all people to marry. He'd ruined his future.

Jim's parents insisted on hiring an attorney to get an annulment. Jim feared his parents, but he went off to be a man. He rented an apartment with his meager savings and bought $20 worth of groceries, mostly canned food, because the apartment refrigerator was no bigger than an ice chest.

On their first night in the apartment, Sandy inquired: "Was it your idea to buy all this canned food?"

"Yes," Jim said proudly.

"Where is the can opener?" She smiled, knowing they'd forgotten to buy one.

Jim ran out to his car and came back with a hammer and screwdriver. Then the two sat down to their first supper as husband and wife. It would be one of the couple's few happy moments.

Once married, Sandy's flip side—ugly and stone-faced—surfaced. She turned out to be bad-tempered and extremely jealous. Perhaps she really didn't love him, Jim wondered, and the new union brought out resentment. Whatever the reason, her ire contributed to terrible, violent arguments.

One of those altercations broke out after Jim glanced at a girl as he and Sandy drove to visit Jean and Dave Beard.

"If you want that so bad, go get it. Go after it," she screamed, smacking him all over—in the head, arms, groin—with her hand.

The car swerved on the highway. After

regaining control, Jim unleashed his own temper and slapped her. She cringed, but gave him a defiant stare.

Jim worked day and night in construction and managing restaurants to put the marriage on solid ground. It paid off; the couple easily bought a home in a quiet neighborhood. Jim tried persuading his wife to get a job, but she showed little enthusiasm. Only once did she acquiesce to working briefly, and that was for a donut shop. Jim didn't know it then, but her only ambition was to stay home and have children. She wanted one of each, a boy and a girl.

Sandy was unpleasable. She resented everything. And every time she exploded, she yanked off her wedding ring and discarded it. Jim and Sandy were parked on the shores of Carter Lake in Omaha the first time she did it. Red with anger after a lovers' quarrel, she pitched her wedding ring into the lake. Never to be found. Another time, she threw her wedding ring in the car. Later, they found it wedged in the metal part of a seat, twisted and badly damaged. Sandy had the audacity to demand another one. Jim gave in, only to have it disappear in the house in the wildest fight of their marriage.

That dispute erupted, Jim later recalled, one summer day while he sat in the living room watching television. Unexpectedly, an ashtray flew at his head from the kitchen. It missed its mark but hit hard against the wall behind him. Without waiting for his reaction, Sandy started smashing dishes against the counters. Unsatisfied with that, she took a knife to the furniture. Slashing. Cutting. Cursing.

When Jim confronted her, she flipped over a small, flimsy kitchen table and yanked a leg off. Jim's knee popped as she swung the wooden leg like a bat. Almost simultaneously, Jim reared back and punched his wife in the face, knocking her out.

That was the last straw. He stomped to the phone and called Jean: "Come get your daughter out of my house. I've had enough." Jim still was very much in love with Sandy, but he couldn't handle the relationship anymore.

Sandy lay unconscious on the kitchen floor when two of her brothers and Jean appeared at the front door. They thought she was dead. If Sandy hadn't twitched, her brothers would have torn Jim apart.

As happens, Jim and Sandy made up. But their turbulent disagreements persisted, especially after David, Sandy's old boyfriend, briefly entered the picture again. Jim was a little wiser by then. It appeared to him that Sandy encouraged the reunion. *THAT* his heart could not accept, and now he hated her.

Ironically, it was Sandy who filed for divorce on June 21, 1973, the day before the couple's third wedding anniversary. Earlier that month, she had informed her mother of her plan to leave Jim because he couldn't produce children, his sperm count was too low; and the arguments were getting worse. Both were true.

"I can't take it anymore!" she told Jean.

Sandy was a restless woman. Within days of filing for divorce, she complained to her brother, Ron, that she was tired of being alone. She needed to be with someone.

"Do you remember anyone from high school who isn't married?" Ron asked.

"Well, there's Steve Harper." Sandy shrugged. "I hear he's doing all right." She didn't know Steve that well, but she used to talk with him in the hall at North High School before the start of history class.

Steve lived a stone's throw away from the Missouri River in a small residential community known as East Omaha. Kids liked to fish the "Muddy Mo" for catfish or sit on its banks to watch tugboats push large barges up the slow-moving river. Adults in East Omaha had little use for the historic river. They still cursed it for the relentless floods of the 1940s, which left most of the area impoverished. Many residents still lived in rebuilt shanty homes with poor plumbing and heating. Steve's family was much better off than most residents.

Steve was quiet and shy. Residents of East Omaha respected and admired the young man because he had more schooling than most adults in the community. They spoke of him with pride: "He's a survivor!" Everyone knew he was going to make something of himself!

Many residents trusted him implicitly. During vacations, they'd leave their homes and vehicles in his care. One family depended on him to look after their retarded daughter when construction jobs forced them to travel around the state. For days, Steve lived in the family's home doing everything for the girl: brushing her hair, feeding her, reading to her.

Now Steve was an aspiring veterinarian attending Creighton University, a prestigious Jesuit school in the heart of Omaha.

Steve had never dated, feeling too insecure to ask a girl out. A woman, especially one as hard as Sandy, was the last thing he needed.

Sandy told her brother she desired to see Steve, but she didn't want to be the one to call him.

Ron volunteered to make the approach.

On hearing of the upcoming date, Jean questioned her daughter's sincerity: "You never mentioned him to me."

Responded Sandy nonchalantly: "Well, I really didn't care too much for him then."

Ron Betten's phone call in June 1973 circumvented Steve's greatest inhibition: mustering the guts to ask a woman out. After reminiscing a bit about North High, Ron muttered:

"You know, Steve, my sister Sandy is getting a divorce and could use a friend. She remembers you from high school. Why don't you call her?"

Steve could not believe what he was hearing. A girl wanted to see him? And who was Sandy, anyway? At first, Steve couldn't place her. Then he nodded. She was the petite blonde he had spoken to before history class.

"Sure, I'll call," Steve said, and requested her phone number.

Steve's parents, Jesse and Eva Lou Harper, were ecstatic when their daughter gleefully screamed that Steve had a date—*WITH A REAL LIVE GIRL.*

The only women Steve had ever known were those who beckoned from billboards, outdoor magazines, or store catalogs. Up close, he had seen them working in the kitchen in elementary school, flirting with boys at North High School, and dissecting frogs at Creighton University biology labs. In his world, they were all the same: cardboard cutouts. Untouchables. At least for him.

He'd never held a girl's hand or kissed a girl intimately. Conversely, he'd never felt a butterfly kiss or experienced a young woman's ardor in the shadows of the school gymnasium during a boring dance.

Love? Romance? Steve had read about them in required literature classes, but, essentially, those emotions were foreign to him.

At the time Steve met Sandy, he was twenty years old and knew absolutely nothing about women. And since his parents were out of town on a two-week vacation, he and his first girlfriend had the East Omaha house all to themselves.

According to Steve, Sandy made the first move and as she maneuvered to seduce him, he asked her what to do, how to do it. His first taste of love overwhelmed him: the feeling; the gratification; the total release, physically and psychologically. The experience—and subsequent love sessions, daily and then twice a week—convinced him Sandy loved him, as she professed she did. No woman gave her body to a man she didn't love.

Some things troubled him about her, though. She constantly asked him to say he loved her. She was very insistent about it. Sandy said it all the time to Steve, and once even claimed she had "really loved" him since high school. Steve was a novice at the game of love, but he wasn't stupid. What about her marriage to Jim Murphy?

"I never loved him," she responded. "I never felt he was a man. You're my man!"

Privately, Sandy thought her new boyfriend related poorly to the opposite sex: He didn't know what to say or how to act. It was apparent to her that his inability to interact frustrated him.

Steve's concern always vanished in bed. What a wonderful feeling to be with her, each wrapped in the other's arms.

"She made me think I was very special," he would say many years later. "She swept me off my feet. Eventually, toward the end of summer, I felt that I was in love with her and could not leave her even if I wanted to."

But as the trees dropped their leaves to prepare for another blustery Omaha winter, Steve, in fact, did leave her, at least temporarily, to concentrate on school. Convinced they were "permanently in love" and "would eventually get back together and marry," he saw no harm in taking a break from the relationship.

Sandy protested. She angrily told friends, "Two weeks after school started Steve slacked off on seeing me. He thinks I'm a threat to his education. He feels he has no time for me. He just has to use all his time for studying. He can't even see me once a week. That's no way for a guy to treat his girl!"

She called him at home. He got mad: "Stop interrupting me!"

"Well, what do you want me to do," she queried, "just quit seeing you altogether?"

"No," Steve said.

"Well, I want . . . you know . . . if we are going to stay as boyfriend and girlfriend . . . I would like to see you and you know . . ."

"Be patient," he requested.

Instead, she gave him an ultimatum: school or Sandy. She pushed to marry immediately.

He planned to marry her, he explained, but not until he graduated in the spring of 1975, when he could "provide for her in the proper manner." He wanted everything right.

Bullshit, Sandy thought.

Steve consulted his mother, who strongly counseled against marriage. She suggested he prod his girlfriend into finishing her education, get a G.E.D., since she'd quit school to marry Jim Murphy.

There was only one other person Steve felt comfortable asking for help, and that was a man he'd met recently, in August. His name was Philip E. Lueck, a thirty-eight-year-old native of Brooklyn, New York, who traveled up and down the Midwest teaching and pastoring. In preparing to teach at Grace College of the Bible in Omaha, the minister had rented—sight unseen —in East Omaha. His family seriously wondered if they'd relocated to a third-world country. Even though the community lacked "sophistication," Pastor Lueck and his wife and their two boys stayed.

Almost everyone in East Omaha attended East Side Presbyterian Church, and it was there that Eva Lou met Pastor Lueck. After church one Sunday, she beckoned him aside to request a favor: Would he please befriend her son. She was worried about him. Steve was a dedicated Christian, she pointed out, but tended to keep to himself. That wasn't good for him. He needed someone to encourage him to be less antisocial. Would he please help? The pastor agreed to shepherd Steve and invited the young man to breakfast at his home every Saturday. There, the two read Scriptures and prayed.

During one of the Saturday morning get-togethers, Steve confided that a girlfriend was pressuring him to marry.

"What should I do?"

Pastor Lueck recommended he concentrate on his schooling: "If this girl is a good thing for you, it will work out."

The next time Sandy called, Steve bluntly told her, "If you want to date another guy, just go out and do it. I don't want to keep you locked in the house."

That was *JUST* fine with Sandy. Break up? FINE! GOOD-BYE! Who needed stupid old Steve anyway!

Sandy took Steve's advice and found another target for her affection: a guy named Jeff, who lived in Council Bluffs, the small city in Iowa across the Missouri River from Omaha. After a few dates that winter, Sandy informed Steve she was in love with her new man.

"I didn't get real upset," Steve recalled. "Jeff had fallen for her. I felt that she was just stringing poor Jeff along, using him against me. They had fallen in love even quicker than I had fallen in love. Jeff was shook up when she told him she would not see him anymore."

By the summer of 1974, Steve was back with Sandy and close to getting a coveted degree. What else could a man ask for? What's more, this time the good times in bed didn't stop with the start of school in the fall. Sandy claimed she saw the light, realized the value of school and a job. She enrolled at a business college to train for secretarial work. Now the lovebirds could study together.

But the experiment failed, miserably. Sandy missed going out and having fun. She couldn't apply herself. She nagged Steve, seriously distracting him from his dream of becoming an animal doctor. Finally one evening while they studied at his home, she said: "You're always working. You remind me of Jim Murphy."

Steve worked himself into a state of blind and violent rage, the culmination of a battle that had been growing in his mind for weeks: Finish school or marry Sandy; read in the library or study with Sandy; spend an extra hour doing research or snuggle in bed with Sandy. His physical craving for her overwhelmed his studious mind. He was hooked. Infatuated, he thought of little else and trembled with jealousy at the idea of letting her go again, even for a few short months while he finished his last year. He couldn't stand to think of who might make love to her or who she might make love to. Why was she so damn impatient? Why did she look for other men? And now, now she's comparing him to Jim Murphy, a guy she hated! Outraged, he reached over and started choking her.

Steve finally pulled his sweaty hands off Sandy's thin neck. She coughed and gasped for air. His heart thumped loud in his chest. He apologized and begged for forgiveness. He didn't want her to be afraid. But it was no use; she left in tears.

Sandy later told friends: "I don't know what made him stop."

It took Steve two months before calling Sandy to make up. He expected her to still be angry and demand an apology. She might even require him to buy her a special gift before consenting to see him. In the end, she'd take him back.

"No way!" Sandy said in an icy tone. "We're through. I'm seeing someone else."

He'd heard that before.

"I'm in love with him."

He'd heard that before, too.

"Steve, I'm going to marry him. His name is Duane Johnson. We're going to get married."

Something in her voice told him she wasn't kidding, everything was really over. Duane Johnson, whoever he was, planned to win over his girl. It didn't make sense.

"How can this be?" he brooded. "*We* were going to get married! I love her. She's only known him a few months. I thought *I* was the only one she loved."

Steve demanded an explanation for her alienation. She listed the long hours at school and constant arguments. Besides, she teasingly replied, Duane was "a taller man." Her husband-to-be stood one inch higher.

Steve heard all of the elucidations but reacted primarily to the latter one. What kind of asinine reason was that? His confusion turned to anger, but she promptly put a stop to his protesting with the one retort that would quiet him. As Steve recollected once, Sandy proceeded to say she had never loved him and admitted dating him strictly for companionship after her divorce. She needed a warm body.

Steve's mind went blank. Hanging up the phone, he wanted to break down and cry. His worst fear had come true: She'd used him. And she had no qualms about saying it to his face. To her, their time together represented a love affair she could move out of as easily as she had moved in. To him, it was the only adult relationship he'd ever experienced. Rejection hurt. It stung as nothing ever had.

What a fool he'd been. Yet, he still loved her. He needed her! He had to do something to get her back.

Steve called Sandy several times in the next few days, each time promising to spend more time with her if she left Duane.

"Please come back!"

"No," Sandy retorted.

Steve didn't give up trying to win Sandy back. When Sandy obtained a respectable job at the Douglas County Legal Office in downtown Omaha—to everyone's surprise—Steve showered her with flowers and candy at work. When that didn't work, he dropped by her job to talk, often ignoring his studies. After work, he waited outside, ready to give her a ride home.

She declined the offers, telling him, "It's too late for us to try and get back together. I'm not going to go back to you." Then she sharply turned away and got on the bus.

The wedding of Sandy and Duane went as scheduled on January 17, 1975, in a north Omaha church, with a handful of guests attending the simple ceremony.

Pastor Lueck encouraged Steve to forget Sandy: "You've got to put the whole thing behind you. She's married now. You can't undo that. Pray the Lord leads you to another woman who will adequately care for you."

His heart and soul shattered, Steve drifted back to Creighton University to finish his final semester.

Ten

DETECTIVE K. G. MILLER rarely carried home a case.

"You don't want to know what I'm working on," he'd tell his wife. "It's safer if you don't know. There are too many crazies out there."

Norma Miller understood: Her husband was behaving like the typical cop acts at home, grumpy and tight-lipped. She'd talked to enough cop wives to write a book about the dismal phenomenon. Norma realized that once in a great while a case posed some danger to a police officer's family because of the seedy characters involved. But she truly doubted the wrath behind the run-of-the-mill murder ever strayed beyond the pungent smell of the deceased.

If anything, Detective Miller practiced his caution almost to a fault. In his view, one miscalculation, one stupid oversight, and it was over, whether it involved a routine traffic stop or serving a warrant in the ritziest neighborhood. He tried thinking of anything that could go wrong. Working on the bomb squad only tended to exacerbate this tendency. Often, the department dispatched him to inspect suspicious packages at department stores or post offices. Long before leaving headquarters, he'd remove his watch and wedding ring. He'd read jewelry sometimes triggered explosives.

Unknown to Norma, her husband had other reasons for keeping her in the dark about most assignments: He detested exposing her to the barrage of human cruelty. The butchers. The charlatans. The weenie waggers. It still amazed him what people did to each other, especially sexually. One callous cynic in the home was enough.

If Detective Miller could help it, his wife always would remain Norma D. Biggs, the innocent Iowa girl he'd met in the mid-1950s while both worked at an Omaha meat-packing plant. When not sneaking looks at each other, he checked the fat content of Spam and she answered the phone for the company doctor. It was while at the packing company that Detective Miller applied to the police department.

Try as he did, the investigator couldn't keep from dragging the death of Chad Shelton home, night after night, to Norma. As a father of three sons, although all grown and on their own, he obsessively talked about Chad during dinner, on the way to the store, in bed. How could anyone kill that baby? How could anyone poison him?

If it was murder, he had to find the killer. And the courts better convict the son of a bitch or he might contemplate a little street justice. He wasn't going to let this one sit in the books unsolved for every new hotshot homicide detective to pick at. And what if one of *THEM* solved the mystery? Over his dead body. He was never dropping this case.

He would solve it for Chad. Chad, he mourned. Sandy, he loathed.

"I have no sympathy for Sandy," the detective told his wife one evening. "I can't see that she's the victim here. Chad's the victim. Duane's the victim. The Beards are victims. She doesn't look like she cares. Maybe she did it?"

Thinking of Sandy angered the detective. He slapped the kitchen counter, shook a fist in the air.

Norma tried calming him before he got so worked up he'd start raving about the court system turning criminals loose. It was his favorite bone to pick.

She agreed Sandy seemed to exhibit as much sentimentality as a rock but reminded her husband that a lack of overt feelings didn't make a person a killer, although, as anyone, Sandy very well could be.

"She's not what she claims she is," the investigator retorted. "She doesn't go very long without a man. She seems to need men."

His own words suddenly froze Detective Miller. From his anger emerged a thought. The words crystallized: BLACK WIDOW! Is that what Sandy was? Did she thrive on devouring her mates: their bodies, their emotions, their pride? Her men appeared to be dispensable, like old shoes. There was definitely a pattern. There was David in high school; Jim Murphy, her first husband; Jeff from Iowa; Steve Harper from East Omaha; Duane Johnson, her second husband. She'd given them all hell. Had she decided to take the next logical step with Duane, murder?

But how did Chad, Sallie, Bruce, and Sherrie fit in? Little Chad had died and the others were not out of the woods yet. Were they inadvertent victims? Or were they included to muddy the waters?

And how had she killed Duane, if she had killed Duane? With what? How could a high school dropout outsmart a slew of medical experts here and at the Centers for Disease Control? Actually, how could anyone elude modern forensic medicine?

The investigator needed to find the answer to the questions floating around in his mind. Even if it meant casting suspicion on all the so-called victims.

Detective Miller drove to the home of Jean and Dave Beard early in the morning. Jean invited him in and offered a lumpy sofa in her tidy living room. She sat in a large wooden easy chair. Dave wandered in and out. The investigator gave no explanation for dropping by unannounced. He just plunged right in.

"Can you tell me about your daughter, Sandy?"

"What would you like to know?" Jean asked cooperatively but a bit puzzled.

"Anything that will help me understand her better."

Not knowing exactly what the detective was after, Jean began with Sandy's childhood.

There wasn't much to Sandy, Jean pointed out. As a girl, she was always hurting herself. If she wasn't bumping her head on the corner of a cabinet, she was tumbling off a bicycle. She seemed accident prone. Not a day went by without Sandy running in the house screaming; "Mommy, I hurt myself. Mommy, I hurt myself."

Sandy kept to herself, Jean continued. Even when disciplined, she said little. An incident came to mind. Jean could not remember what her daughter did wrong, but Jean had ordered her into a dark closet until she apologized or said something nice. Minutes turned into hours without a peep. Reluctantly, Jean let her out.

In high school, Sandy never spoke of a career or college. Nothing enticed her. She didn't write poetry, read history books, or play a musical instrument.

"The only thing she wanted was to look

pretty in nice dresses," Jean said with a chuckle. "She liked kids, too. She was a good mother and she kept her house spotless."

"How did she meet Duane?" Detective Miller wanted to know.

Jean looked down at her pale hands on her lap, then whispered, "She stole him from Sallie."

That didn't surprise Detective Miller.

Jean explained. The Beards infrequently invited guests to dinner—it was difficult enough feeding their own large family—but they made an exception for Sallie one winter night in 1974. As the studious one, Sallie spent hours in her room doing homework until it was perfect. Even though she loved books and school, at seventeen she'd gotten interested in the opposite sex, too, and Dave had mentioned a nice "boy" he'd hired to help sell car parts. His name was Duane Johnson and he really wasn't a boy anymore; he'd recently turned twenty.

There was nothing extraordinary about Duane, he was just a friendly, regular guy with a ready smile. His parents had lived in the Omaha area since 1936. His father, Edwin, earned good money building homes, but liked raising a few cattle to make sure his six children ate well. On occasion, Duane visited his father to help slaughter a cow.

Sallie had asked to meet Duane, who had no inkling why he'd been invited to dinner, but, never one to shun a good home-cooked meal, he happily accepted. From the beginning of the modest meal of meat loaf and scalloped potatoes, Jean could tell the youngsters found each other attractive. But the matchmaking soured when a guest arrived, as unwelcome as a cheetah at an antelope watering hole. The guest was none other than Sandy, who fixed her eyes on Duane. Within a few days, he selected the blonde, instead of the brunette. Sallie proved no match for her older sister.

"Sallie and Duane made a nice pair," Jean told the investigator wistfully.

Dave spoke for the first time. Tears filled his eyes.

"Duane was a good kid, a real good kid. He drank beer and smoked but he stayed out of trouble. I loved that kid."

"He had his own father but he liked to be around Dave," Jean offered. "Sometimes, he'd show up for work before we were up. Can you imagine that?"

"That's right," Dave jumped in. "I'd find him curled up in my car, asleep like a little puppy. You know, he called me Dad before he knew I had good-looking daughters."

Detective Miller stared at Jean sternly: "You told me the first time I talked to you that Duane and Sandy got along pretty well, but I understand Sandy was pretty rough on men."

Jean acknowledged the detective's remarks, but contended the relationship between Sandy and Duane was amicable. At least most of the time. In the days prior to the poisoning there did seem to be friction.

"They were mad at each other over something," she said. "I don't know what it was about. All I know is Sandy wasn't with Duane during the Septemberfest festival. You see, Duane asked his boss if he could use an empty lot near the festival during Septemberfest. His boss said sure. Duane made some pretty good money charging people to park there. He let us park free."

"You have no idea what was wrong?" the detective persisted.

"No. All I know is they weren't getting along."

The room grew quiet.

Detective Miller eyed Jean. She was holding back, he could tell. He didn't speak. Sometimes, silence drew people out.

Jean finally looked up to divulge her inner thoughts. "I think Sandy had something to do with it. Some way, somehow, Sandy had something to with Chad and Duane dying."

Jean's revelation caught the detective by surprise: He hadn't expected such candor. But from the little he knew of Sandy, he understood why her own mother might speak disparagingly about her.

"Sallie thinks so, too," Jean said with a nod. "When she was in the hospital, she told me she thought Sandy was involved. She told me, 'I can't prove it, there's no way to prove it, but she had something to do with it.'"

Recently, Jean went on, she'd confronted Sandy with her suspicion. She'd asked, "Did you have anything to do with all this?"

"No," Sandy responded, without showing anger or indignation at the accusation.

Such nonchalance often implied guilt. In Sandy's case, it could be meaningless since she and her sisters refused to open up to their mother, partly because she'd abandoned them, although temporarily, during the breakup of her first marriage. The girls confided in Dave, their stepfather.

Dave desperately wanted to pose the same question, he admitted to the investigator, but feared the answer. What if Sandy said yes? What then? She was far from the perfect daughter, but he loved her just the same.

"I plan to ask her," he said, "someday before I die."

"Do you really think she could poison anyone?" Detective Miller asked.

Jean did not believe her daughter had committed the actual poisoning—she loved children too much—but she did believe she had contributed to it in some way. She observed that Sandy had always brought the family grief and more than likely invited the latest calamity on everyone.

Whatever role Sandy played in the lemonade horror, the Beards agreed, they doubted anyone could make her talk. Judging from his limited conversations with Sandy, the investigator tended to agree. In his line of work, he had met plenty of people with invidious personalities. They seldom went a day without turning someone's pristine water into smelly mud.

Detective Miller asked how Sandy had made the family suffer.

Jean pointed to a scar just under her right eye. "One of her old boyfriends did this. A shotgun pellet hit me right here. That was years ago. He's still in prison."

"Damn computers," Detective Miller cussed under his breath. He'd run Sandy's husbands and boyfriends through the computer and nothing had come up. Shootings were felonies. It had to be in the computer.

Eleven

AFTER INTERVIEWING JEAN and Dave Beard, Detective K. G. Miller hustled to police headquarters to run all the names through the computer. Once again—not surprisingly, though—the computer was down.

"Shit," the investigator muttered.

Following his personal philosophy of "Why walk when you can ride," the detective jumped back in his car and drove the few blocks to the courthouse to search for Sandy and Jim Murphy's divorce. In the past, divorce files bulged with dirty laundry. Not anymore. No-fault divorces reduced them to half a page of euphemisms. With the help of a clerk, he located the file. It contained nothing the investigator didn't already know.

Detective Miller returned to his office. By then, the computer was up. He typed in: Murphy, Jim. Nothing appeared, indicating Murphy was "clean." But how could that be? Sandy and

Jim had thumped on each other all the time. The investigator asked another detective to try it. Same results. It would be several weeks before he learned police were never called to the Murphys' knock-down-drag-out fights.

The telephone book contained several Jim Murphys. With the help of tidbits from the divorce file, however, the investigator soon obtained telephone numbers and addresses for the *right* Jim Murphy and his family from the state Department of Motor Vehicles.

No one seemed to know Jim's whereabouts. His parents claimed they had lost track of him after his marriage to his high school sweetheart disintegrated.

"We knew it would," Jim's father snapped.

The last time they saw him, they said, he was depressed, ashamed.

Once more, Detective Miller sat down at the computer and typed the name Harper, Steve. The screen filled with criminal vitals:

"HARPER, Steven Roy, Cau/Male, DOB: 4-18-53
2403 North 19th Street, E.O., 5'9", 155 lbs.,
2411 North 19th Street, E.O., Brown hair,
Blue eyes, OPD# 79556, SS# 508-70-4068,
FBI# 101-105-K1, NPCC# 30916.
Father, Jesse HARPER.

Possible Vehicles: Turquoise, 73, Chevy
  Stepside."

"Look at this!" he yelled to no one in particular as he jumped up, knocking over his chair
in his eagerness to search for the police reports
in the homicide-assault files. Cursing the antiquated computer, he wondered why the "hit"
failed to come up the first time.

After a few minutes, he located a thick
"Crime Against Person" folder containing numerous police reports. It was an old shooting,
case No. 44983H. Picking up the top report, he
glanced at the box listing the victim. It said
"Betten, Daniel Carl." His eye moved down to
the box for suspect information: "Harper,
Steven."

"Shit!"

He hurried to the next report. Victim:
"Jean." Suspect: "Harper, Steven."

Detective Miller flipped through more reports, looking for other victims: "Johnson, Sandra." "Johnson, Duane."

"Son of a bitch," he cursed again. "He attacked the whole family."

The shooting intrigued the investigator—violence was violence—but it appeared a far cry
from the unsolvable medical mystery he was
currently pursuing. What troubled him most, at
that moment, was Sandy.

Detective Miller recalled asking her about

old boyfriends. None of them, she swore, would wish to hurt the families.

The detective searched through his brown spiral notebook containing his notes on his interview with Sandy. What were her exact words? There they were. He'd asked her about Steve. Sandy had depicted him as "a quiet person not prone to violence. He did not drink, smoke, or use drugs." In fact, she had said she knew him only as a "peaceful person."

"What a crock of shit," he said out loud. "A peaceful person, my ass. Is she trying to hide something?"

One thing Detective Miller detested were people who deliberately misled him.

The investigator went back to perusing case 44983H. It provided the bare facts: dates, ages, heights, weights, weapon. The file could not, however, convey the malice of the moment.

Three years had elapsed since the shooting. Back then, Jean and Dave Beard and the five youngest siblings had resided in a two-story eight-room house on Camden Avenue in north central Omaha; the girls slept upstairs, the boys downstairs. Living away from home were Dan, Sandy, and Ron. Sandy had not gone far: She and Duane occupied the house across the street from the Beards.

Rather than celebrate after graduating from Creighton University in the summer of 1975, Steve plunged into a depression. All along, he planned to wed Sandy after finishing school. His mother and father suffered, too, from his frustration and growing sarcasm.

On the night of June 20, 1975, Steve's temper exploded over a minor disagreement with his father. Steve yelled, screamed like a crazy man, a rabid dog. In the heat of the argument, he threatened to shoot Jesse.

Dazed, he drove off with intentions of killing himself, to put an end to the emotional merry-go-round. Instead, he parked his old, white pickup truck on a hill overlooking the corner house rented by Sandy and Duane.

Steve fidgeted behind the steering wheel as he leaned forward and peered into the damp, cool night for movement, any sign of his old flame. It was very late—one in the morning—but he knew Sandy had to come home sometime, and he was not leaving without emphatically demonstrating that no one—except him—could have her. She belonged to him.

About ten minutes past one, the stalker's angry red eyes squinted, then widened with excitement: A faint streetlight below illuminated a blue mid-1960s Chevy slowly driving up to his old girlfriend's house. Six people hopped out of the car: Sandy and Duane; Sallie and her husband-to-be, Bruce; and Dan and his date. The three boisterous couples were returning from a fun evening: They'd seen a movie and had stuffed themselves with pizza. Now they planned to play cards and have a few drinks at the Beard residence.

In an instant, Steve's pickup swooped down and screeched to a halt in the middle of the street. Startled by the urgency of the offending noise, the revelers stopped in their tracks.

Dan recognized the driver.

"Leave my sister alone," he shouted into the night air. "She doesn't want to see you anymore. Just leave, don't cause any trouble."

"What are you doing here, Steve?" Sandy demanded bitterly as she walked up to the driver's side of the truck. "What do you want?"

Steve mumbled something about his father but Sandy couldn't make out what he was trying to say. His eyes darted wildly from side to side. They steadied upon seeing Duane approach the truck. Steve grabbed the woman's forearm to yank her out of the way, for she stood between him and his prey. Duane lunged forward to protect his young bride from the crazy man in the truck.

"Don't!" Sandy shouted at her husband, pushing her body backward to keep him away. She would have welcomed his chivalry if it weren't for the .410 shotgun she'd spotted lying on her ex-boyfriend's lap. While the newlyweds struggled with each other, Steve thrust the shotgun out the truck window to find his mark. Duane was close enough to the vehicle to reach over his wife and push the end of the barrel downward.

The blast ruptured the night, causing everyone to scatter. Metal pellets ripped deep pock marks out of the asphalt, before ricocheting in all directions. After a moment, only the puffs of soft white smoke rising from the shotgun, dared move.

The explosive ruckus stiffened Jean and Dave Beard, who sat in their living room watching television. Dave headed his potbelly upward off the couch and onto the front porch. He'd barely opened the wobbly screen door when Duane flew by, almost knocking him over.

"The son of a bitch is trying to kill me! Call the cops!"

Duane ran up the stairs, skipping several steps on the way; into a second-floor bedroom; out a window facing the back of the house; and down a set of rear steps. His fleeting body disappeared into the night.

The enraged ex-beau jumped out of the truck and found Sandy crouched behind the pickup. He pointed the shotgun at her from five feet away.

"Where did he go?" he asked.

She didn't answer.

Dan stopped running near a tree in his parents' front yard, turned, and hollered: "What the hell you trying to do?"

Stooping to a soldier's combat position, the jilted lover fired blindly at the voice coming from the tree. The blast tore through Dan's left shoulder. Some of the pellets missed and embedded themselves in the wood siding of an adjacent house, waking up the occupant, the wife of a biker. She grabbed a loaded handgun and cautiously moved toward a front bedroom window.

"Help me, I've been shot!" Dan yelled. "Help me!

About the time Dan collapsed on the lawn, Jean looked out the living room window: "What's going on out there?"

Steve whirled in the direction of the voice and fired a third time.

The window shattered, turning her wrinkled face and graying hair bright red with blood. One of the pellets pierced the skin near her right eye. After burrowing through the flesh and exiting at the back of her head, it lodged itself in a hall wall. Other pellets riddled a lamp shade.

By now, the biker's wife could see the gunman in the street near the pickup truck, firing indiscriminately. She wanted to shoot but her window was stuck. No matter how hard she jerked at it or swore at it, it would not budge.

Dan staggered to his feet, his bloody left arm dangling from his body. Steve fired a fourth time, striking him in the left side of the head and face. Dan went down a second time.

"You shot my brother!" Sandy screamed. "You shot my brother! You killed my brother!"

Without saying a word, Steve tossed the shotgun into the bed of the truck and sped off.

As everyone came out of hiding, Dave

reached inside the front door and dialed 911. A
cruiser's emergency flashing lights soon lit up
the neighborhood and Dave ran into the street
to meet it. He recognized the officer. It was Lollipop, so nickamed for his penchant of sucking
on lollipops and Tootsie Rolls. The corner of
33rd and Camden was out of his district, but
the officer thought he'd come by in case the re-
sponding units needed help.

"It was Steve Harper who done the shooting," Dave told Lollipop after pointing out the
four spent shotgun shells on the street.

"I think I know where he lives," the officer
said. "I'm going after him."

A medic unit pulled up for the injured and
transported them to the Lutheran Medical Center.

Dan was extremely lucky: He survived, and
with no apparent brain damage. Jean suffered
multiple facial cuts and pellet wounds, but the
injuries were hardly noticeable once all the
blood was wiped off her face. A little blood
could make a person look pretty gruesome.
Nevertheless, she'd been lucky, too: Half an
inch higher and a little more to the left and one
of the shotgun pellets would have punctured
her eyeball.

About a quarter to five that morning Jean
and Dave gathered their wounded family at the
hospital and went home, sans Dan, who faced
an indefinite stay at the hospital.

Everyone was still awake at home. The children, frightened and sniffling, rushed to the front door.

"Is Dan okay? Is Dan okay?"

Dave assured them their brother was doing well, but he explained that doctors still needed to remove plenty of pellets. Some wouldn't be so easy to get out, especially one or two near an eye.

"What happened?" asked Roger, a curious fourteen-year-old. "Why was he shooting?"

Dave glanced at Jean and took a deep breath: "Sandy dumped him. Your sister dumped him for Duane and he's mad. Plain and simple."

"Will he come back?" Roger wanted to know.

Dave didn't mean to alarm the children, but he believed in being as honest as possible with them.

"I hope he doesn't," he replied, "but I don't know."

Duane thought he had not heard the last of Steve, but his nature was so easygoing that the entire incident appeared comical, now that the shooting was over. The prospect of another jealous attack had come up a couple of hours earlier in the hospital waiting room.

Almost rhetorically, Duane had asked, "I wonder what's going on?"

"You're a target for assassination," Dave replied with a bit of melodrama.

"Why?"

"You married Sandy!"

"Well, it's his loss and my gain," said Duane with a laugh.

"It ain't going to be your gain if you're dead, fool."

"I guess," concluded Duane in a more serious tone, "I'll have to keep looking over my shoulder."

Sandy said little about the shooting at the hospital. And once home, she simply offered, "I've brought another episode on the family."

After giving the children soda pop to settle them down, Jean and Dave ordered everyone to bed. Sandy and Duane—the target of Steve's wrath—silently walked out the front door, past the blood-smeared lawn, and across Camden Avenue to their house. At that moment, love didn't feel so wonderful.

From reading the police reports on the shotgun attack, it was clear to Detective Miller the family feared Steve would return to finish the job. According to the file, the Beards repeatedly contacted the police that morning to find out if Steve was in custody. He was not.

The shooting turned the Beards into a family of frightened turtles, prepared to withdraw their heads at the slightest foreign sound. Jean and Dave peeked into the street every time they heard a vehicle door closing or the roar of a pickup going by. The children refused to play outside. The family ventured out only to visit

Dan at the Lutheran Medical Center. They planned to stay all morning, but left after an hour, for doctors needed to extract a dozen or more pellets.

Back home again, the Beards caught Sandy and Duane leaving their house with a handful of their possessions. The young couple intended to go into hiding from Steve. They contemplated staying with Duane's parents on their acreage for a few days, then looking for another secret hideaway. In any event, the two said, they wouldn't be in touch for the time being.

Late in the afternoon, the Beards telephoned the police again, hoping to hear they had nothing to fear. Unfortunately, that wasn't the case. Steve's pickup had been found abandoned in a parking lot at Creighton University. Under the seat of the truck, police discovered a twelve-inch butcher knife with an eight-inch blade and a .22-caliber bolt-action rifle. The shotgun was missing.

"He just disappeared off the face of the earth," the desk sergeant told the Beards.

Fortunately, the human mind tends to blur or simply erase unpleasant experiences. Within a week or so, the shooting seemed in the distant past, not forgotten, but remembered more as a bad dream that surely would not reoccur. Since Steve appeared to have backed off, the Beards went picnicking, a favorite pastime all around the Cornhusker State. But the peace of mind

Jean and Dave relished in the first days of July that year was short-lived.

The white envelopes—which would become numerous in the coming weeks—arrived at their home, but were for their daughter. Some were addressed to "Mrs. Johnson," while others to "Mrs. Murphy." Although Jean didn't know what the letters contained, she could sense the evil inside and strongly suspected they were sent by the jilted lover.

One of the envelopes troubled her far more than the others. When she found it, she shivered as if an arctic wind had blown over. That one had not been delivered by the mailman: She knew because it was not postmarked, yet it was in the mailbox. Clearly, the person who put it there did so in a clandestine manner, probably under the cover of nightfall.

For weeks, the letters sat around the house, emitting bad karma. Jean's opportunity to learn what was inside came one early August day when Sandy called from her secret hiding place to say hello.

"You've got some letters here," Jean said impatiently. "I think they're from Steve."

"I don't want to have anything to do with them," Sandy responded coldly.

"Well, what do you want me to do?" Jean asked.

There was a pause at the other end of the phone.

"Open them and find out what they are."

Jean carefully unsealed the letters. They all contained the same message: "Duane will never have Sandy." Her hands trembled.

"What does he want?" she wondered. "Why doesn't he go out and find another girl? Why is he doing this?"

Sandy was nonchalant about the whole thing: "Oh, just throw them away."

Their brief conversation ended with Sandy promising to call again, sometime.

Jean immediately telephoned the Omaha police to document the threats. After assuring her that every patrol car in the neighborhood would be paying "special attention" to her home at night indefinitely, the desk sergeant dispatched an officer to Camden Avenue to pick up the correspondence.

Steve was relentless.

In mid-August, another menacing letter arrived at Camden Avenue. Jean's face lost all expression. The missive, postmarked August 12, 1975, was addressed to "Mrs. Murphy (Betten)." The envelope contained no letter, only several color pictures cut out of a witchcraft magazine. Jean could hardly believe what she held in her hands. She summoned her husband: "Dave, look at this. It really looks like he's losing his mind. There's something wrong with him."

"He's a sick son of a bitch," Dave said, glancing at the demonic material. "He's got to be put away. Let's get the hell away. I want to move out of state."

This time, Jean didn't bother calling the police. She simply stuffed the letter in a box in the closet, with some old photographs.

Detective Miller searched among the shooting reports for the various letters. The final few pages mentioned Steve's eventual arrest—almost a year later—but there was no sign of the letters.

The detective reread the reports, finally finding a note explaining that the correspondence had been put in the property room. He took the elevator downstairs to the basement and handed the evidence room attendant a piece of paper with the case number written on it. The attendant disappeared into the warehouse. Shelves and bins overflowed with fireplace pokers, coats, liquor, burglary tools, forty pairs of dice, wallets, two cans of tomato juice, bumpers from hit-and-run accidents, three hundred rifles, and bloodied shirts and boots. All remnants of the pains and sorrows of personal tragedies.

After a few minutes, the attendant reappeared: "Nothing there."

"What do you mean there's nothing there? The file says the letters went to the property room."

"They did," the attendant added, "but they were destroyed to make room for evidence in more current cases."

Detective Miller understood the predicament faced by the property room—with crime rising every year—but it angered him just the same. He hoped it wasn't an omen of the way this investigation would proceed.

Detective Miller looked at his watch: It was too late to call the Department of Corrections to ask about Steve's imprisonment. Riding the elevator back to his office, he wondered what made Steve explode so violently. What made him send the letters? It couldn't be simply over a girl. What was behind his extremely possessive nature?

After the shooting, Steve ditched his truck and walked to a friend's house near the university. The next day, he moved to the home of a relative. In August, about the time Jean and Dave Beard opened his last venomous dispatch, he boarded a bus south to Tulsa, Oklahoma, where he found a warm bed with an uncle. In his new, milder environment—far from the pressures of his parents, school, and Sandy—he realized how badly he needed help.

On the morning of September 30, 1975, Steve picked up the telephone and dialed a number he'd obtained earlier in the day. When a receptionist answered, he requested to speak to Dr. Lynwood Heaver, a Tulsa psychiatrist who specialized in medical hypnosis. The receptionist explained that she would be happy to set up a consultation appointment, but first was required to fill out a "Prospective Patient Telephone Inquiry" form. After obtaining his name, she asked about the nature of his problem. She listened for a while, then jotted down, "Bad burns—felt paranoid about them." The receptionist instructed Steve to come in at ten on Wednesday October 8.

Steve hoped Heaver could relieve his depression and obsession with Sandy. He'd considered hypnosis out of desperation: He felt out of control. He couldn't believe how violent, mean-spirited, he had become and how easy he was finding it to hurt people. He could justify his hatred for Duane, but almost shooting his father was beyond comprehension. And where was his rationale? He was driven to see Duane out of the way, but the consequences had not occurred to him: Someone would probably get hurt and that, in turn, would make him a criminal, a felon. How could he be so naive, stupid, to think no one would come after him, to hold him accountable?

"Why did you come to see me?" Heaver asked when he and Steve sat down privately.

As the patient recounted his predicament— cleverly leaving out the shooting—the doctor took notes on a form entitled "Consultation Interview: Initial History." Under "reasons for consultation," Heaver wrote, "Wants to learn self-hypnosis to help get over feeling of depression . . . to help him study." On a second page, he added, "Broke off relationship . . . wants not to think of her again. Has read several books on self-hypnosis but can't put himself into it . . . she dropped him." And in heavy black letters, he noted: "Already in trance!"

Anxious to know more about the young man sitting in front of him, Heaver had him take the Minnesota Multiphasic Personality Inventory (MMPI), a test requiring days to weeks to analyze.

Before the appointment was over, the psychiatrist hypnotized Steve to help him purge Sandy from his thoughts. In a second session the following morning, the doctor hypnotized Steve a second time to help him relax.

It would be years before the doctor knew if his treatment had helped. The man with the scars—apparently a transient just passing through—did not return.

Steve felt infinitely better after seeing the psychiatrist, and he would have continued his visits if it weren't for the cost. Shortly after the consultations, he left Oklahoma for Missouri, to see other relatives for about a month before going home in December 1975.

The shooting remained a thing of the past until July 10, 1976, the day a uniformed officer stopped Steve on his motorcycle. A computer check revealed a year-old warrant charging him with "shooting with intent to kill, wound, or maim," a felony. It was time to pay the piper.

Steve's parents hired a well-known Omaha attorney named David Herzog. The lawyer didn't think his client stood much of a chance and recommended he plead "no contest" and place himself at the mercy of the judge. Such a plea meant the defendant did not admit guilt, but believed he would be found guilty if tried by a jury. Steve took the advice. To further his cause, he penned a letter to the court, apologizing for his anger:

> I have deep remorse for what I did. I offered and still would like to help the Bettens for the damages I inflicted on them. I learned a bitter lesson in the game of life. Now, I hope to be able to continue the normal life I had. I cannot take the crime I committed on the Bettens away, but I am deeply sorry and will help them in any manner to try and help alleviate some of the grief I brought to them, also to redeem myself for the grief I caused my family.

On December 6, 1976, Eva Lou and several relatives packed the courtroom to show the judicial system Steve had a loving, supportive family willing to carry him to better days. Herzog stood and told Douglas County District Court Judge Donald J. Hamilton, "I can't really offer anything in mitigation as to how Mr. Harper chose to resolve the problem with a girlfriend, and that's just exactly what the substance of the event and transaction was that he stands convicted of today. I think he has learned his lesson the hard way."

Raising both eyebrows, the judge grumbled:

"There are arguments pro and con as to whether or not the penal complex is a deterrent to anyone, but I am evidently from the old school because I still feel it is. This young man must learn that using a weapon is not the way of solving his problems, and especially in this instance, where there was no question that two innocent people were injured as a result of his felonious act. Therefore, it will be the judgment and sentence of the court that the defendant be imprisoned in the Nebraska Penal and Correctional Complex for a period of one to five years at hard labor."

The sentence stunned Steve. The embarrassment he'd brought on his family particularly distressed the East Omahan: He had never intended to put them through such a painful public process. He'd let them down and set the worst example for his brothers and sister. He'd also let his community down: Instead of fame, he had brought shame.

With Steve put away, Jean and Dave Beard eased into their simple, uneventful existence as apartment managers.

Sandy settled down to realize her dream of being a simple housewife with children, one of each.

Sallie married Bruce, her tall, handsome escort on the night of the shooting on Camden Avenue.

As Detective Miller prepared to go home, he puzzled over the files and the many entwined players. Everything seemed to revolve around an ex-husband; an incarcerated, jealous ex-boyfriend; and a temperamental, fickle woman.

Twelve

In Detective Miller's mind, Sandy Johnson still stood out as the best suspect. She seemed the most likely killer because she'd made the lemonade and she did not tell him the full story about her relationship with men. Usually, people held back information from the police for one of two reasons: to protect themselves or someone else. Was either of those the case here? Maybe Sandy murdered her husband knowing her ex-boyfriend-turned-criminal would be blamed? It had happened in other cases before.

Steve Harper looked good, too.

The former suitor undoubtedly had a motive to harm the family, and the shooting demonstrated his capability for indiscriminate violence. But he was in prison, according to Jean Beard. Or was he?

Detective Miller telephoned the Nebraska State Parole Office in Omaha. A parole officer who identified himself as Bill Hendricks informed the detective that it would take a few hours to dig out Steve's prison file, but he was somewhat familiar with the individual. The inmate, he explained, became eligible for work-release in July 1977 and was paroled in mid-November 1977, with parole ending three months later.

If the dates were correct, Steve certainly was free when the Sheltons and Johnsons were poisoned.

"Where is Steve now?" the investigator asked.

Hendricks wasn't sure, but remembered that at one time he applied for a travel permit to attend Iowa State University in Ames in preparation for veterinarian school.

As soon as he finished talking with Hendricks, Detective Miller contacted the Iowa Bureau of Criminal Investigation to ask if it could send an officer to Ames to ascertain if Steve had attended the school. A couple of hours later, the bureau reported back. Steve had applied for the fall quarter of pre-veterinarian school on June 4, 1978. However, in an August 3, 1978, letter to the institution, he requested his enrollment be delayed: He was having minor surgery on a burned hand.

Burned hand? Detective Miller wondered.

"The letter doesn't say how he burned it," the bureau agent replied.

Curiously, Steve's correspondence with

Iowa listed a home address in Carter Lake, an odd-shaped patch of land near Omaha on the Nebraska side of the river. The property, technically, belonged to Iowa. Steve had never lived there, leading the detective to theorize the East Omahan gave the address to avoid paying out-of-state tuition.

Showing that Steve didn't travel to Iowa meant nothing by itself. To implicate Sandy's former lover, the investigator needed to prove Steve was physically in Omaha about the time of the deaths. And, preferably, he had to do it without alerting Steve.

Detective Miller recalled his old off-duty job at Harold's Market in East Omaha, a mom-and-pop store where most residents of the area shopped for groceries. He figured Steve would shop there if in town. His hunch paid off.

Store records revealed that Steve wrote two no-account checks in August 1978, one for ten dollars and the other for fifty-five dollars. On September 12, two days after the poisoning, he had walked into the business to cover the bad checks with cash. The employee who waited on Steve the day he settled the accounts told the investigator that the young man had been coming into Harold's once a week prior to paying off the checks. She last saw him on the twelfth.

An old hand at constructing paper trails, Detective Miller next rummaged through the department's records bureau for anything involving individuals with the last name of

Harper. He found a single case. It pertained to a Michael Harper, a sixteen-year-old who'd crashed his motorcycle on September 6. Michael turned out to be Steve's brother. Apparently unable to come by police headquarters to pick up an accident form to notify the state of the mishap, Michael had sent Steve. The form bore Steve's signature next to the date: September 7.

What luck. Steve had had to be in town.

By midafternoon, the state parole office delivered a copy of Steve's thick file to police headquarters. Detective Miller hunched over his desk and submerged himself in a lengthy interview Steve gave the prison staff. Raw with emotion, the interview chronicled the East Omahan's life.

Now the investigator was beginning to understand why Steve had clung to Sandy Johnson, why she meant so much to him.

Steve's sad misfortune erupted one April day when he was nine. That day, Steve, a brother, and several friends met at a dump near their home to play. One thing led to another and the youths started a fire to burn snakes slithering about. One of the boys thought it might be fun to pour gasoline on the blaze. Seconds later, Steve was on fire, his entire left side ablaze like a human torch. Neighbors looked in horror as Steve rolled on the ground. When he finally stood up, flesh dripped from his body.

"Oh my God! My son's on fire!" screamed Steve's mother hysterically.

Not long before the accident, Eva Lou had undergone minor surgery and with the excitement of the fire, all of the stitches pulled out, requiring her to return to the hospital. Complications delayed the healing, and it would be at least a week before she could see her suffering son.

Within moments of the fire, Steve lapsed into shock and remained in that condition for several days at Children's Hospital in Omaha. Doctors gave him little chance to live. In the 1960s, rarely did persons survive severe burns over half of their body. Even with burns on sixty-five percent of his body, mostly to his left side, Steve *did* live, and after coming out of shock, the face he saw at his side belonged to a grandmother. She held his small hand day and night.

The fire ravaged his body. What used to be smooth, beautiful skin now consisted of grotesque, discolored lumpy tissue stretched in all directions, like globs of half-dried Elmer's white glue. Since he beat the odds, an attempt would be made to repair the damage.

Steve's memory of that nightmarish summer became one big painful blur. In spite of strong medication, it hurt when they wrapped him up in gauze bandages to protect what remained of the epidermis and it hurt when they unwrapped him to rebandage him. It even hurt when they fed him fluids to keep him from dehydrating.

Debridement caused the greatest agony. The process involved applying a wet dressing to a burned area. As soon as the dressing dried, it was peeled off, along with dead tissue. In spite of the drugs they gave him, his entire body shook with excruciating pain. The mere thought of seeing the debridement crew walk in the room horrified him.

Steve felt abandoned: He wondered why his parents allowed the hospital staff to hurt him so much. His young mind—clouded by the tragedy —couldn't comprehend what was going on.

After recuperating, Eva Lou diligently helped care for her son. It was the hardest thing she ever had to do. The procedure to repair the damage seemed so cruel to her. No mother should have to go through that. After leaving her son's room, she would weep uncontrollably.

It was a miracle Steve lived, but there was no time to fully appreciate it. The medical focus quickly shifted to whether he might lose a limb or a specific body function. Severe burns often stunted a child's growth. Would this happen to Steve? Could one side of his body develop naturally into that of a man, while the burned side remained that of a nine-year-old? Certainly, medicine had come a long way from the days of covering fresh burns with black mud and cow dung. But scars and damaged tissue still presented numerous medical problems.

Steve underwent at least thirteen operations and skin grafts before leaving the hospital. Months later, he returned, reluctantly, to the same sterile environment for several more operations.

For the next five years, he would go through therapy at a rehabilitation center, yet it would not end there. Even into the 1970s, he'd need a skin graft or two.

Detective Miller stopped reading the prison interview long enough to grab a fresh cup of coffee. In a way, he felt sorry for Steve. The detective wondered if *he* could endure such pain. He read on.

The fire completely changed Steve: his appearance, his relationship with his family, his outlook on life, his view of himself. The most glaring difference concerned the disfiguring scars. They began at the left cheek and extended down the side of the neck. At the chest, they meandered to the left arm before stretching to the stomach and leg, where they stopped, abruptly, at the knee. Raw and unprotected, the flesh screamed at the slightest sensation, particularly extreme temperatures.

In time, the body would heal. But for the immediate future everything—sleeping, sitting, walking, dressing, smiling, crying—would be painful.

Steve hated to touch the scars; the lumps brought back vivid memories of the fire and sent shivers up and down his body. He cringed, too, whenever anyone reached toward him. That was an involuntary response brought on by months of debridement.

Most of all, the fire devastated his psyche in ways not readily apparent to those who knew him. Under his quiet, unpretentious demeanor lurked emotional chaos.

The mental degeneration process began the day he left the hospital's burn unit. Once home in the privacy of his room, Steve could see the complete outcome in the mirror. He didn't like what he saw; it repulsed him. Occasionally, he caught the scent of burning flesh. It made him sick to his stomach.

The scars nagged at his self-confidence. At school, he no longer mingled with other kids; their "gawking" bothered him. Unfortunately, this pattern of avoiding relationships persisted through junior high and high school.

Often, classmates encouraged him to try out for football or basketball.

"Sports," he'd say, "aren't for me."

What no one realized was that Steve was not going to participate in any activities that required him to take off his clothes. Even in the summer, he wore long-sleeved shirts.

His reluctance to take part in anything except classwork created a niche for him that he

The Johnsons: Duane and Sandy with daughter, Sherrie, and son, Michael. Taken shortly before Duane died.

The home of Duane and Sandy Johnson at 5422 Fontenelle Boulevard. The window to the far left was used by Steven Harper to enter the house.

Top: Sandy Johnson when she was three years old.

Bottom: Sallie Shelton.

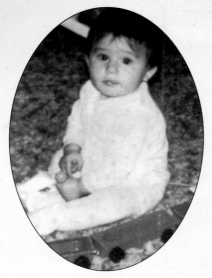

Chad Shelton playing with a wooden train.

The home of Jean and David Beard in 1975 when
Steven Harper ambushed the family.

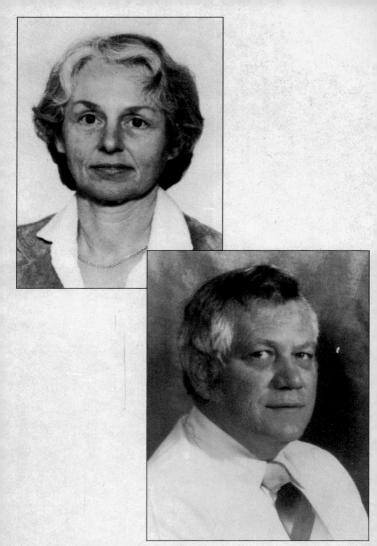

Top: Dr. Renate D. Kimbrough of the Centers for Disease Control in Atlanta.

Bottom: Omaha Police Department Detective K. G. Miller.

did not relish but could not change. Adolescence is a time when students are the cruelest to each other. The slightest difference—skin color, weight, pimples, a lisp—cuts a person out of the mainstream. And Steve knew he was now "different."

At church, too, Steve shied away from meeting people. He was polite to parishioners and his mother's friends, but he engaged in few lengthy conversations.

The older he got, the more withdrawn he became. Much as he tried to forget his physical appearance, everywhere he went people reminded him in not so subtle ways. At a movie theater one evening, he heard a girl whisper to another girl, "Look at that kid's face!"

He later told a friend, "I felt like a hideous, repulsive creature who should be locked away forever."

It was no wonder he'd never asked a girl out.

Despite the tragedy, Steve's parents expected him to do well in school. His sister and brothers needed a role model. Nothing could absolve him of that duty.

Steve rose to the challenge. Upon returning to school after the fire, he performed at the top of his elementary class. At North High, he concentrated on subjects he'd need to enter veterinarian school: history, foreign languages, and biology.

Even as a boy, Steve dreamed of becoming an "animal doctor." He loved animals and pleaded with his parents for pets of his own. How could his parents deny such ambition, especially since they'd never finished high school.

Steve asked only for a pet or two, but before long, cages of all shapes and sizes peppered a partially wooded field near their house. He raised pheasants, sheep, quail, turkeys, chickens, geese, and the usual cats and dogs.

Seldom did a day go by that he didn't spend hours grooming the animals and fowl after watering and feeding them. Steve grew so attached to his animals that it wasn't unusual for him to pass up invitations from friends on their way to the Missouri River to fish.

When Steve graduated from high school, Jesse and Eva Lou Harper couldn't be prouder: Their son possessed his passport to prosperity. The good life. His graduation picture held a place of honor atop the living room hutch, where they could admire it from an easy chair. Seeing their son graduate made ten years of paying medical bills worth it. The Harpers lamented only one thing: Steve had never seen a psychiatrist as part of his treatment. It wasn't done back then.

Steve harbored great misgivings about his appearance, but he'd grown up to be a slender, rather average-looking man with sparkling blue eyes and reddish-brown hair. Some scars still protruded from his face and neck, but they were dramatically less pronounced than right after the fire.

In the fall of 1971, Steve enrolled at Creighton University. Tuition was high, but he chose the private school because it offered Latin, a requirement for veterinarian school. To help make ends meet, he sold his animals and accepted a part-time job working for a Creighton secretary.

He never intended to shoot anybody after getting his biology degree, he told the prison staff. He'd been depressed, angry.

"This girl I knew in school had gotten divorced and she began seeing me," he explained. "She, as I see it now, used me as a whipping post, but we dated and she kept wanting to get married. I developed a lot of feelings for her and she went and married this other guy."

From reading the prison file, Detective Miller could tell Steve's hard-luck story had moved the prison staff: Instead of housing him with the general population, they assigned him to the trustee dormitory, giving him more freedom to roam throughout the institution.

The sympathy appeared to pay off for society. At the end of the file, the investigator came across a one-page letter from a counselor who evaluated Steve's mental stability. The counselor wrote:

It is felt by this counselor that Mr. Harper has a mature outlook toward his incarceration, and will present no problems. It is felt that Mr. Harper has the maturity and insight to successfully reenter the community upon release from the institution.

Thirteen

WHERE WAS JIM MURPHY? Hiding at home? On the lam in another country? How could his parents not know his whereabouts? Was *he* the killer?

Detective Miller was pondering those questions late the afternoon of the last Friday in September when a secretary gestured that she was transferring a call to him. It was Bill Hendricks of the state parole office. In examining Steve's file more closely, Hendricks explained, he'd come across a list of jobs the inmate had held once out of prison. According to the job history, Steve had worked at a local medical research center at one time.

"A research center?" The big investigator almost fell out of his chair.

"Yes," Hendricks responded. "I thought that might be important to you."

"It sure is! What's the name of the center?"

"The Eppley Institute."

Detective Miller was sure he was on to

something. Research facilities employed an assortment of drugs and overflowed with pills and jars of unusual compounds.

After talking with Hendricks, the detective called John Wiley of the health department. He should know of this latest development.

"John, this is K.G. I just found out that one of Sandy's old boyfriends worked at the Eppley Institute."

There was a long pause.

"John? Are you there?"

"Yes, I'm here." Wiley felt rather stupid.

"Some employee at CDC called this morning to inquire whether any of the victims ever had exposure to the Eppley Institute," Wiley said shyly. "I thought she was crazy."

The CDC employee had been Dr. Renate Kimbrough. She'd refused to give up. Since her initial tests, she'd spent almost every waking minute trying to solve the riddle. At home—after feeding her family and meeting all her other domestic obligations—she researched toxins and their effect on various organs of the body. In the laboratory, she stared into her binocular microscope until headaches forced her to step away.

That morning, she thought she spotted what she'd been looking for. Examination of actual tissue from Duane's brain, heart, and kidney disclosed nothing but normal cells. And an analysis of microscopic slides of tissue belonging to Chad revealed no abnormalities. A portion of liver tissue from Duane, however, excited the physician-toxicologist.

Bleary-eyed, she studied the lobules, the small units that make up a liver. Liver-attacking toxins, Kimbrough knew, damaged different parts of the lobules, and in Duane's case the cells in the center were ravaged. That was significant, consequential, because she had seen damaged cells like those before: not in poison victims but in research work. She couldn't remember, just then, when or where she had seen them, but she had. Now she guessed the victims' livers had been destroyed by a very exotic chemical.

"Where would they come in contact with potent chemicals in Omaha?" she asked herself, trying to control the rush of adrenaline.

There was only one research facility in the entire city of Omaha. Kimbrough immediately picked up the phone and dialed Wiley's number. At the time, she was unaware of a criminal investigation.

When the epidemiologist came on the line, she explained lobules and her suspicions of the involvement of a research chemical.

"You know, Mr. Wiley, this is not the sort of chemical you get at a corner drugstore."

One thousand miles away, Wiley shook his head, bewildered: "What did lobules have to do with it? What was she talking about?"

Wiley listened, politely, to several more minutes of scientific explications, but nothing the doctor said made sense. Not to him, at least. Where was the connection?

"Did any of the victims have anything to do with Eppley?" Kimbrough had finally asked.

Wiley didn't know, but he doubted it. Her theory, he told her, appeared a long shot.

Wiley was still shaking his head in disbelief at the end of the conversation. In Atlanta, Kimbrough could feel his cold shoulder.

Wiley's account of Kimbrough's observations seemed to confirm—for the first time—that Omaha police were on the right track. IT WAS MURDER. Detective Miller considered getting in touch with Kimbrough. Instead, he hurried into Lieutenant Burchard's office, thinking that a little more old-fashioned legwork would resolve the mystery. He was wrong. He would regret ignoring her scientific expertise.

What the investigator had uncovered was very incriminating. Steve's job at Eppley could be a coincidence, but the investigation was far too important to take chances. To minimize legal mistakes, Lieutenant Burchard requested the help of the Douglas County Attorney's Office. Understandably, little was said about the health department's attempt to get the prosecutor's office involved in the early stages of the case.

Detective Miller made plans to rendezvous that night with Douglas County Deputy Attorney Sam Cooper, the leading prosecutor of murder cases in the county. The two men knew each other from previous homicides and worked together well, especially since they both preferred meeting over a Scotch or a beer.

To Cooper, the biggest drawback to working with Detective Miller was his penchant for storing explosives in the trunk of his car. At times during investigations, the prosecutor rode in the detective's car and feared someone rear-ending them, triggering an explosion so powerful there wouldn't be enough fingers and toes left to bury. Cooper realized, too, he might have a lot of explaining to do if the investigator lapsed into a mischievous mood. Once, the two were assisting another county in a case requiring scuba divers. After the divers dove deep into a lake, Detective Miller drove to the far end where he could not be seen and threw in several explosive devices. On Cooper's side of the lake, the divers popped up vibrating like church bells, wondering what had happened. On Detective Miller's end, dead fish shot up like a giant fountain. What a way to fish!

Detective Miller had to drive to a home in west Omaha to meet with Cooper. When the investigator arrived, he found the deputy prosecutor and a friend cleaning a giant red, white, and blue hot air balloon they'd purchased a couple of years back from a U.S. Air Force officer.

Cooper listened to the investigator's spiel—knowing his office had committed itself to working with police—but at the conclusion of the presentation he was less than convinced of foul play. Earlier in his career, he would have been quicker to label a death murder. It wasn't until he almost had obtained a murder conviction—in a suicide—that Cooper learned to reserve judgment.

Endless were the ways people killed and elaborate were the methods they used to conceal the evidence. Once, investigators discovered a man in his house with all the doors locked and a fatal gunshot wound to the head. Everything pointed to a suicide, but the weapon was missing. Detectives were stumped until one of them looked up the fireplace chimney in the room the man died. To mask the cause of his death, the deceased had tied a rubber cord to the gun. After he shot himself, the cord yanked the gun up the chimney.

Fourteen

DETECTIVE MILLER RAN hot and cold. One moment he was certain Sandy or Steve had poisoned the families, the next he wasn't. Some of his doubt had nothing to do with either suspect. He simply had trouble believing one human being could intentionally harm so many people. Potentially, ten persons could have died, including another infant.

That weekend, the detective's notion of Steve began shifting permanently, persuading him Steve could be the killer, not some innocent animal lover caught up in a weird coincidence.

On Sunday, October 1, Jean Beard contacted the investigator. She had something for him. Did he have a few minutes? Even though it was his day off, Detective Miller put on a suit and drove to her home. He figured it must be important for her to call on a weekend.

When he arrived, Jean met him at the front

door and handed him a short, thick envelope containing a threatening letter from Steve. She told him it had been sent after the shooting.

The detective waited until he got home to open the letter. Inside, he found a stack of cutouts from a demonology magazine. One consisted of a paragraph: "When pursuing an unwilling victim, the spirits would assume the form of a trusted figure, such as a father confessor or bishop (in the case of a girl) or a nun or some young beautiful woman of unimpeachable reputation (in the case of a man)."

Obviously, Steve thought an evil spirit intended to capture his soul through Sandy.

Another picture portrayed a blond woman on a bed with a red-horned devil on top of her. Printed on the woman's face were the initials S.B. (for Sandy Betten). A short phrase under the picture read: "The pleasure of a demon lover . . ."

A series of four cutouts depicted a bare-breasted, blue-eyed blonde growing horns while slowly turning into a hairy demon. The first one in the series had the initials S.B. written on the woman's neck.

The venomous demonology cutouts made Detective Miller realize he was dealing with a possessed man—a twisted mind—not a sane, rational person inclined to cringe at the thought of poisoning an entire family. In Steve, he saw a modern-day Othello, a character mad with a jealousy that had survived the penitentiary.

Fifteen

EMBOLDENED BY THE witchcraft letter, Lieutenant Foster Burchard decided to go after Steve Harper: corner him and sweat him into divulging what he knew of the poisoning.

First, the lieutenant needed to probe Steve's mind. What were his fears? His weaknesses? Was he streetwise? What *would* make him cough up the truth? Should police lean on him? Give him the good-guy-bad-guy routine? Or should they jolt his brain with crude photographs of Chad Shelton's autopsy?

To find out, Lieutenant Burchard ordered Detective Miller to deliver all the prison reports and the police file on the shooting to Omaha psychiatrist Emmet Kenney. He'd helped police in these mind games before. The lieutenant was interested in one thing: the best way to induce Steve to talk once he was in handcuffs.

After reviewing the material, Kenney surmised that Steve appeared to be a paranoid schizophrenic who held Sandy and Duane responsible for all his misfortunes. After allowing her to get emotionally close to him, he felt Sandy had betrayed him in marrying Duane, something Steve could not stand. As to Duane, Steve hated him outright for stealing Sandy. Kenny's conclusions mirrored the results of the Minnesota Multiphasic Personality Inventory test given to Steve in Oklahoma, but the test's existence was still unknown to police. Sadly, Steve would have discovered his own mental instability if he had continued seeing the hypnotist in Oklahoma. Sandy and her charms appeared to be the impetus for his violent anger, but his mental problems grew out of a psychological weevil that promised to erode his mind.

Bullying Steve would not work, Kenney told Lieutenant Burchard. Neither would the good-guy-bad-guy routine. The psychiatrist suggested Steve be interviewed by a single person with a disarming personality, someone Steve might feel he could trust.

That cut Detective Miller out: The object was to get Steve to talk, not scare him to death. As the lead sniffer, he would have liked to be the first to confront Steve, but he was seasoned enough to know he needed to step aside.

The psychiatrist also offered two caveats:

- The interrogator should not wear dark glasses. Trust hinged heavily on eye contact.
- The door to the interrogation room

should be left open to avoid giving Steve the feeling he was psychologically locked in.

Only one homicide detective truly fit the criteria: Greg Thompson. He could put a slug to sleep. His laid-back personality misled killers into believing they could take advantage of him. They were wrong. His puffy but smiling eyes noted every nervous twitch and inconsistency. Thompson turned out to be quite a serendipitous selection. He'd gotten the East Omahan to open up after his arrest for the 1975 shooting.

Lieutenant Burchard wanted to arrest Steve at once but lacked the evidence to obtain an arrest warrant. He mused over his options and decided to request a search warrant for Steve's house. Judges were more likely to issue search warrants than arrest warrants. When the warrant was served, the lieutenant hoped, his creatively diligent men would entice Steve to "visit" police headquarters. There, Detective Thompson would take a crack at him.

To ensure that their zeal did not leave them on shaky legal ground, Lieutenant Burchard met with Cooper and other representatives of the Douglas County Attorney's Office. The consensus favored seeking the search warrant since Steve had the motive and the opportunity to commit the crime.

On October 3, the police convinced a judge to issue the search warrant. Detective Miller was elated. His long-awaited meeting with Steve seemed imminent.

About midmorning, a detective telephoned Steve's home. It was an old trick: When the target picked up the phone, officers knew he was home and moved in. But no one answered. The detective called again. Still no answer. He tried a third, fourth time. No answer.

Authorities faced a dilemma: The warrant had to be used that day. When no one answered the phone at 1:30 P.M., a caravan of cars drove out of the basement of police headquarters and headed north. A few minutes later and about a mile from the airport, it turned east into East Omaha. Once past Harold's Market, the caravan curved right to a cluster of giant trees that partially hid a small brown rambler with white trim. A narrow wooden board with Steve's address carved into it was nailed to a fence post. Out piled several detectives, including Lieutenant Burchard, Sergeant Parker, and Detective Miller. They were accompanied by criminalist Don Veys, prosecutor Sam Cooper, and epidemiologist John Wiley.

Search warrant in hand, Detective Miller cautiously walked around a rusty bicycle on its side in the front yard and up to the front door. A large padlock held the wooden door closed. He went to the back of the house. The rear door was also secured with a lock. He would have liked to kick down the door, but didn't. Instead, Sergeant Parker walked two doors south to the residence of Jesse and Eva Harper. A leery Jesse unlocked the house only after being assured the place wouldn't be torn apart, as he knew police sometimes enjoyed doing. Lieutenant Burchard stood outside with Jesse and one of his Doberman dogs while detectives entered the home.

Inside, investigators found a dusty but tidy house, sparingly furnished. It didn't look lived in.

On a desk in the front room lay a chemistry book entitled *Organic Chemistry*. Various notes on lined paper were strewn about. One said:

"B.J. died in three to four days. No. 2 . . . lost much control in rear legs. . . ."

The initials didn't match the name of any animals owned by the Harpers, as far as investigators could tell. Nevertheless, the scribbles hinted at home experiments. In the same room, on a shelf, the team found a small brown bottle and a corked glass vial with the number 24 written on it. The vial contained traces of a white crystal. Was that the poison?

Careful not to obliterate any fingerprints, detectives gathered the book, notes, and receptacles.

A search of the kitchen produced a pair of surgical gloves and a bag full of one-pound containers of sulfur potassium nitrate, aluminum powder, potassium chloride, and charcoal. The chemicals, Detective Miller knew, could be combined to make an effective explosive.

On the kitchen table sat what appeared to

be a message with the name and address of a couple in Pasadena, Texas. A detective confiscated it.

The search moved to a detached garage, a white A-framed structure a few yards from the house.

"That dirty rotten bastard," Detective Miller muttered after a quick look around the garage. "He ought to be hung with a short rope."

To Detective Miller it appeared that Steve had used his small abode to experiment before administering the coup de grace at the Johnson home. Five commercial-variety wire rat cages, complete with feeders, covered the garage dirt floor. There were no animals, dead or alive, but rat droppings littered the cages, as well as parts of the building, indicating the rats, at times, had run free. A detective took samples of the droppings and of a clear liquid in one of the feeder bottles.

Although the notes in the house and the cages in the garage seemed to confirm everyone's suspicions, the search team found nothing linking Steve directly to the poisoning—at least not enough for an arrest warrant. Homicide detectives seized nineteen items, but their significance and usefulness as evidence was unclear. Not even the residue in the bottle and vial appeared plausible as the poison.

Was Eppley a coincidence? Were the cages merely an extension of Steve's biology studies?

Detective Miller wasn't buying that theory.

The search left him frustrated, unfulfilled. Now *HE* was a man possessed. What did Steve use? How did he do it?

Before leaving, Lieutenant Burchard ordered his men to search the grounds for dead animals. On the north side of the garage, detectives stumbled across a small grave with a homemade wooden cross over it. They dug it up. Inside a plastic bag they found a smelly, decomposing short-haired dog.

"A family pet," Jesse offered. "It died of heartworms."

The investigators didn't believe him and started pulling the animal out for examination. Angered, Jesse grabbed a shovel and threatened to start swinging. His Doberman growled. To avoid further confrontations, Sergeant Parker telephoned the veterinarian who had treated the animal. The vet confirmed Jesse's account, and the examination was scratched.

On their way off the property shortly after 3 P.M., Sergeant Parker turned to Jesse:

"Where's your son?"

"Out of town . . . in Beaumont, Texas."

Of course, the sergeant didn't believe him.

Steve, in fact, *WAS* in Beaumont, experiencing a serenity he had not felt for years. Gone were his cravings for Sandy and gone were the demons that had begun visiting him after he left prison.

Once his love turned to hate, the solution was obvious. Why hadn't he thought of it be-

fore? The insidious wheels of his mind helped
him figure out what he needed to do to get back
at Sandy for all the misery he'd suffered. She
deserved it, the witch! And no one would ever
know it was him. Oh, someone might suspect
him—because he and Sandy had gone through
a few lovers' spats while dating—but no one
could ever prove it, not in a million years. He'd
planned it so well. Not everything went perfect,
but perfect enough. Not only was the fantastic
poison he'd discovered virtually unknown in the
world, it was undetectable in the body after
death. It just vanished. Poof! He'd committed
the infamous perfect crime. Yes, the previously
unaccomplishable perfect crime. Not even Scot-
land Yard could figure this one out.

The best part, the very best part of his bril-
liant scheme, was yet to come. The deaths were
far from over. Down the road, years from now,
more of those who drank his secret would die.
Without him lifting another finger. They'd suffer the same fate as the others. And no one
would ever guess he had done it.

Yes, his had been the wrong heart to break,
the wrong heart to set on fire.

By day, Steve now worked as a laborer for
Daymar Corporation, an Omaha-based company installing $100,000 in navigational equip-
ment at the Jefferson County Municipal Airport
just outside of Beaumont. By night, he strolled
the hot, sandy beaches of the Gulf of Mexico or

leisurely read his mail on the bunk bed of a mobile home he'd borrowed from an uncle.

Quite a few relatives wrote to him, but it was easy picking out his mother's letters. They came in light blue envelopes with a dark blue edge. Written on stationery with the phrase "What's New with Eva Lou . . ." engraved at the top, her letters were short, only a few paragraphs, but they arrived frequently to keep Steve informed of the mundane: a fish fry at "Gram's" or a layoff in the family. Most of the time, she'd end her letters with "I am praying for you. God bless you. Love, Mom."

Since leaving Omaha for Texas in mid-September, his mother forwarded mail, unopened, from a young prison groupie named Mary. The woman had started corresponding with Steve in prison, after obtaining his name from a friend in the institution. Steve and Mary had never met, even after he got out, but she still wrote to him and occasionally telephoned his home. Mostly, though, she was a paper girlfriend whose letters reinforced Steve's feeling that he had done the right thing to Sandy and her family. Women teased so cruelly.

In a September 19 letter, Mary rambled about trying to pick between two jobs, then said: "And as far as Mike goes—he's no competition for you! He's trying super hard though with all of the letters, candy, and presents! Why don't you 'court' me like that? Dave came over tonight expecting to sleep with me, but I told him that I'm going to have to start sleeping alone again! He wasn't happy . . . because he knew you had something to do with the decision." She ended it with: "P.S I'M HORNY! 'Cum' satisfy me sometime."

In a September 25 letter, Mary exploded over Steve's going to Texas without telling her. She'd learned of the trip when she called Steve's home one evening. She wrote: "Well, for all I care right now—fuck you and forget you!!!"

If Mary had known what Steve had done less than a month before in Omaha, she would have chosen her words more carefully. In truth, she would have stopped writing altogether.

Mary represented everything Steve hated about women. It was beyond his comprehension how they shifted their love so easily from one man to another. Did they ever stop to think they were hurting someone? Stupid women! Ugly women! He didn't care if he ever met another. Maybe Mary deserved what Sandy got, the same medicine? Maybe he should pay Mary a secret visit to teach her a lesson. The bitch!

Steve preferred letters from his grandparents, like the one he received in the first days of October, almost to the day that the Omaha police had searched his East Omaha home. That was a good old-fashioned one, void of hate and demands. Their short note simply told him that they had killed eighteen chickens, cleaned them, and dressed them to eat. No more, no less.

Sixteen

THE LONGER THE Shelton-Johnson case went unresolved, the more Detective Miller abused the homicide filing cabinets. Every time he walked by the files, he'd shove his big shoulders into them, like he used to do to opponents in high school football games. He was in such a foul mood the morning after the search of Steve's home, in such a rage, he smashed into the cabinets repeatedly, then threw a wooden chair across the room. Everyone ducked. The chair smashed against a wall, sending the wooden legs rattling across the floor.

Irked he'd been unable to uncover any evidence, Detective Miller drove to the Eppley Institute to rattle some cages. He wanted to know, exactly, what Steve had done as a research technologist. Secrecy was no longer important. The Harpers, more than likely, had contacted their son, wherever he was.

Eppley proved another miserable dead end.

Institute officials contended, adamantly, that Steve had never worked on toxic experiments, only on a project in which laboratory animals were fed "sodium saccharin."

The investigator demanded to see Steve's personnel file. Officials obliged. Steve's job specifically involved:

1. Handling rats.
2. Preparing various diets.
3. Feeding rats.
4. Doing autopsies, particularly to prepare urinary bladders and kidneys for further processing.
5. Assisting in biochemical experiments relating to the urinary bladder.
6. Observing all safety rules.

While reading the file, Detective Miller helped himself to Steve's employment application. His eyes stopped on question G. It asked: "Have you ever been convicted of any offense (other than a minor traffic violation with a fine of $50 or less)? No _____ Yes _____ If yes, please explain." Steve had left it blank. And apparently no one at Eppley had pursued this.

According to the file, a Dr. Terence Lawson had supervised Steve. Forcing himself to be pleasant, the detective asked to speak with Lawson. He could, he was told, if Dr. Lawson was in town.

Detective Miller hated doctors, despised them: the real ones and the pseudo ones who used the title to call attention to the years they'd gone to school. Pompous asses.

The trip to Eppley wasn't a total loss. The investigator learned the rats and cages in Steve's garage probably came from there. One of Steve's jobs required him to transport rats to a variety of institute facilities. Recently, an employee had taken a head count and discovered quite a few missing.

About 1 P.M., Detective Miller headed to the south Omaha office of veterinarian Dr. Arthur Strobehn. He felt compelled to examine the records of the dog found buried in Steve's yard. To his disappointment, the records, indeed, proved the animal—a forty-seven-pound, seven-year-old female beagle hound—had died of heartworms.

"A dog of this age has little chance of recovering from heartworms and treatment is expensive," Strobehn explained.

Detective Miller returned to his car, spitting and cursing. Before driving off, he opened his spiral notebook and wrote "Female dog checked positive for heartworms. No other workup. Heartworms would cause jaundice. Doubtful dog was poisoned."

There was only one thing left to do: Find Steve Harper. He had all the answers.

Over the next couple of days, Detective Miller spent most of his time hiding among the trees and vacant houses of East Omaha, trying to get a glimpse of his suspect coming and going. As he spied every passerby, the investigator mulled over what made people go bad, rotten like soft apples on wet ground. What made them selfish to the point where even a child's life meant nothing.

Father Flanagan's memorable words came to mind: "There's no such thing as a bad boy . . ."

"Wrong, Father Flanagan!" thought Detective Miller. He knew, firsthand, that the world was full of bad boys: young ones, old ones; white ones, brown ones. And bad girls, too.

At night, the detective moved closer to the Harper home to count the vehicles that traversed their street. He wrote down the make and color of every car and truck that stopped at the Harper residence. Then he compared the information to a list of vehicles registered to the Harpers. Only one family vehicle appeared missing: a 1970 red two-door hardtop Chevrolet. Maybe Steve was driving it and an all-points-bulletin should be issued? Or maybe it was parked outside the residence of the couple in Pasadena, Texas? The community was on the outskirts of Houston and just west of the town of Beaumont.

On Friday, October 6, police requested that Pasadena plainclothes officers cruise by the couple's home on Alastair Street to look for vehicles with Nebraska plates. They found none.

At the end of that week, Detective Miller

was out of leads and out of ideas. All week he'd hit dead ends. He felt like a posthole digger who had come across a rock with no outside edge. Everywhere he inserted his spade, it bounced off.

Seventeen

FOR THE SECOND SUNDAY in a row, a telephone call yanked Detective Miller out of despair. This weekend's revelation, though, promised to be the fortuity he had been waiting for to break the case wide open. It was 2 P.M., October 8.

The caller identified himself as Ron Betten, one of Sandy Johnson's brothers. He wanted to pass on a story he had heard at church that morning.

Ron and some of his brothers and sisters worshiped at Full Gospel Assembly Church of Council Bluffs in Iowa, across the Missouri River. So did Eva Lou Harper and one of her sons. Since the death of Chad Shelton and Duane Johnson, the two families avoided each other on Sundays: They'd look away when their eyes met and made it a point to sit in different pews. Sometimes, the families couldn't help but greet each other since they attended the same Bible study. After the study, people talked more about the tension between the Bettens and the Harpers than the Christians and the Romans.

Ron told the investigator that the Harpers were forced to take a dog and a cat to a veterinarian clinic in Omaha. The animals died.

That didn't seem like new information to the detective. It sounded like a rumor spun from the discovery of the animal grave at Steve's house.

It was no rumor, Ron assured the gruff voice on the phone. The animals, he insisted, ended up at the Northwest Animal Clinic. They were poisoned. YES, POISONED!

That caught Detective Miller's full attention.

"When did the animals die?"

"Sometime in August," Ron said. "About a month before Chad and Duane died."

"Where's this clinic?"

"On Seventy-second Street."

The homicide detective thanked Ron and hung up. Sitting in his living room, he wondered what happened to the corpses. The pets could be the critical link. Toxicology tests might identify the poison. But a dreadful thought occurred to him: What if the animals had been cremated?

The next day, Detective Miller walked into the animal clinic the moment it opened. The detective introduced himself to the veterinarian, Dr. Ernest B. Summers.

"Do you recall an incident a month or two

ago where someone brought in a poisoned dog and cat?"

"Yes, I do," the vet said.

"Can you tell me a little about them?"

"Sure, let me get their worksheets."

Summers talked as he read from his file: "Mrs. Eva Lou Harper brought in the Doberman pinscher on Aug. 7. The pup appeared to be approximately eight weeks old. The dog's name was Levi and it weighed ten-to-twelve pounds. It was black-and-tan in color. It eventually died. Mrs. Harper had no idea how the dog could have gotten poisoned."

"How did it die?" Detective Miller asked.

Summers painted a gruesome picture. Again, he spoke from notes: "When brought in, the dog was drooling and going through seizures; every muscle was in seizure. It was running a temperature of about 105. A dog's normal temperature is 101.5. Atropine was administered because it was suspected he might have organic-phosphate poisoning. That treatment was repeated twice on Aug. 7: 6:15 P.M. and 7:30 P.M. On Aug. 8, the dog was treated with antibiotics to prevent secondary infections."

Recalling the dog's ordeal visibly upset the veterinarian.

"On the morning of Aug. 9, the dog started bleeding from the nose; it had a blood-clotting problem. The dog was given more medication. By noon, the dog's pink gums turned pale, anemic. About 2 P.M. the dog required a blood transfusion to survive. By then, the dog was vomiting. A donor dog was found to collect blood for a transfusion, but the Doberman died at 3:30 P.M."

It was inescapably clear to Detective Miller: Chad, Duane, and Levi had died an identical, torturous death. It had to be the same poison. But what was it? What the hell was it? This was no accident. And only God truly knew the condition of the survivors.

While the dog underwent treatment, Summers continued, another member of the Harper family carried in a cat—a gray-and-black eight-pound male named Cleops—after finding it crying and throwing its head back. The cat could not stand up or walk, but it was not bleeding. Cleops died not long after it came in.

"Were autopsies performed on either animal?" Detective Miller wanted to know.

"No," the vet responded, "no one requested them."

"How were the animals disposed of?" Detective Miller finally asked. He was determined to recover them, if possible.

The dog and cat were handled like any other dead animals: Their corpses were placed in a plastic bag in the clinic freezer to await pickup by the Nebraska Humane Society. The humane society removed Levi and Cleops on Aug. 10. Summers had no idea what happened to the carcasses after they left the clinic. He suggested the investigator contact a Ron Hennington of the humane society.

Glad the animals hadn't been cremated by the vet, the detective drove to the humane society on Fort Street. He was told that all dead animals were kept in large coolers and three times a week Haulaway Inc. scooped them up and delivered them to a landfill at the western outskirts of the city. When Detective Miller expressed an interest in exhuming the dog and cat, Hennington got a curious expression on his face. He pointed out that one thousand five hundred to two thousand animals had been deposited in the landfill since August 10.

Detective Miller refused to give up, especially after hearing, firsthand, how the mysterious poison had ravaged its victims. He was hot on Steve's trail and he meant to make him pay for what he did.

At 2:30 P.M., the detective visited Haulaway Inc. He was led to a man named Denny Dranke.

"You want to do *WHAT*?" Dranke asked. "You've got to be kidding."

Dranke offered one in a million odds against locating Levi and Cleops. At the beginning of each day, a bulldozer dug a trench thirty to forty feet deep and by 6 A.M. landfill employees shoved all the carcasses to the bottom of the hole. After covering them with dirt, the day's trash—approximately one hundred tons—was dumped on top of the animals. Bulldozers then capped the trench with another thick layer of dirt.

Recovering the animals was not impossible, Dranke explained, but very improbable.

Detective Miller understood all that, but he wouldn't be able to sleep if he didn't make every effort. He went up to the landfill.

Employees told him that the chances of pinpointing the exact spot where a trench was dug on a certain day and digging down to find a specific animal were very slim. Besides, most of the dogs and cats had probably long since decomposed.

Levi and Cleops would have to rest in peace.

Eighteen

SILENCE, IN THE WORLD of homicide, implies guilt —at the very least—making Steve more culpable with each passing day of the investigation. Where was he?

Detectives had interviewed his acquaintances. Steve didn't react. Detectives had inspected his home inch by inch. Steve didn't protest. Wouldn't an innocent man come forward—with an attorney, if need be—to clear things up and get the cops off the family's back? And what of his family? They had displayed no outrage at police suspicions and seemed to have done little to persuade Steve to surface and face the horror of his emotional weakness. Obviously, Steve had no intention of turning himself in.

The deaths of Levi and Cleops gave Detective Miller an opportunity to confront the Harpers to further gauge their sentiments and pose questions geared to help investigators plan their next move. On the morning after failing to retrieve the carcasses, he went to East Omaha. A stoic Jesse met him at the front door. Asked about the poisoned animals, Jesse shrugged with ignorance. He knew nothing about the pets; he had not taken them to the clinic. Detective Miller inquired about Steve. Jesse parried. Detective Miller persisted. Where was Steve? Jesse stood his ground, telling the detective he knew only about himself. The investigator gave the much smaller man a hard stare, one that would make most men take a step backward. Jesse stood his ground and stared back. The investigator left.

A couple of blocks from the house, Detective Miller pulled his car to the side of the road to record the encounter in his notebook: "Tried to talk to Jesse Harper. Would not say anything . . . Asked about dog to NW Animal Clinic. Said he didn't take it. Very hostile."

Since Lieutenant Burchard was off for a few days, Detective Miller reported back to Deputy Chief Jack Swanson, who thought the poisoned pets tipped the scales in favor of charging Steve. It was possible the East Omahan was not the poisoner, reasoned the deputy chief, but it would be negligent to allow him to roam free if he was. If Steve had killed, he was a very dangerous man. He might kill again. Swanson felt obligated to resolve the impasse. The way to do that, it seemed, was to charge Steve and legally detain him.

About 10:30 A.M., Swanson met with Detective Miller, Cooper, and County Attorney Knowles. In reviewing the case, the men agreed there were ample reasons to charge Steve: He was the jilted lover; he had attacked the family in 1975; he was in town at the time of the poisoning; he worked at the Eppley Institute; and his family's pets died much like the victims.

However, everyone also understood that the incriminating facts were only circumstantial. There were no eyewitnesses linking Steve to a poison, let alone the crime. Moreover, nobody knew what had killed Chad Shelton and Duane Johnson. What was the murder weapon? The bottom line: A jury probably would not convict Steve.

In their own minds, though, the four men swore Steve probably had killed Chad and Duane. No one could ever convince them the victims died from some "funny" disease. What most compelled the group to favor charges—*demanded* they file charges—were the surviving victims. Did Steve hold the key to saving them? Not necessarily an antidote, but information that could help treat them? How would anyone know unless he was caught and questioned? The county attorney ordered Cooper to prepare warrants against Steve.

Intoxicated with mistrust for Sandy Johnson, Detective Miller badgered Cooper to prepare charges against her, too. He hoped that detailing on paper her turbulent history with men might convince the higher-ups of a conspiracy. He sincerely believed she had been aware that Steve had planned to harm her husband. The detective wasn't sure she knew the full scope of the murderous plot, but he thought she contributed to the tragedy somehow. It wouldn't have taken much to set off Steve's love-crazed mind; Sandy merely had to pretend she was bored with Duane. Cooper emphatically rejected charging Sandy.

"Forget it," he told Detective Miller. "Maybe she did something recently to provoke him, but there is absolutely no proof she conspired with Steve."

Rather, Cooper accused his friend of simply not liking the woman.

By 8:30 the next morning, the warrants were ready: Steve faced two counts of first-degree murder and three counts of poisoning regarding Sallie and Bruce Shelton and Sherrie Johnson.

Few people outside law enforcement were aware the deaths were the subject of a criminal investigation. Once the health department had proclaimed the city safe from any contagious disease, the media had focused on more sensational news. The serving of the search warrant on Steve's house, however, created serious information leaks, and journalists began hearing rumors of a criminal angle to the tragedy. Neither Police Chief Richard Andersen nor Lieutenant Burchard would confirm such an investigation, but veteran police reporters smelled something cooking. Fresh meat, as they sometimes liked to say. By the time the judge signed the arrest warrants, the media were hounding the homicide unit. Reporters came by several times a day, hoping for a slip of the tongue. The chief could have ordered limited access to the detective section, but the move would have caused more speculation. Instead, when a reporter strolled in, homicide investigators pretended to be busy on old hard-to-solve cases. Or they'd open up their *Playboys* and pretend to be wasting the taxpayers' money.

But on the morning of October 12, a Thursday, authorities let the cat out of the bag at a news conference at police headquarters. County Attorney Knowles and Deputy Chief Swanson were the "moving lips," as journalists called official spokespersons. Detective Miller dropped by out of curiosity but stood inconspicuously at the rear of the room, away from the cameras. Speaking into several microphones, the deputy chief read a prepared statement:

ON THURSDAY, 14, SEPTEMBER 1978, CHAD SHELTON, AGE 11 MONTHS, DIED AT CHILDREN'S HOSPITAL IN OMAHA, NEBRASKA. ON FRIDAY, 15, SEPTEMBER 1978, DUANE JOHNSON, 26, DIED IN CLARKSON

HOSPITAL IN OMAHA, NEBRASKA.
SEVERAL OTHER MEMBERS OF THIS
FAMILY WERE HOSPITALIZED WITH
SIMILAR SYMPTOMS. THERE WAS
CONCERN AROUND THE CITY THAT
THIS WAS SOME TYPE OF COMMUNI-
CABLE DISEASE. THIS HAS SINCE
BEEN RULED OUT BY HEALTH DE-
PARTMENT AUTHORITIES. BASED ON
CERTAIN INFORMATION RECEIVED
AND DEVELOPED BY THE OMAHA PO-
LICE HOMICIDE DIVISION, INVESTI-
GATORS OPENED A CRIMINAL INVES-
TIGATION IN CONJUNCTION WITH
THE DOUGLAS COUNTY ATTORNEY'S
OFFICE. AS A RESULT OF THIS INVES-
TIGATION THE DOUGLAS COUNTY AT-
TORNEY'S OFFICE HAS ISSUED A
FIRST DEGREE MURDER WARRANT
FOR STEVEN ROY HARPER, WHITE
MALE, 25 YEARS OF AGE, LISTED AD-
DRESS: 2411 North 19th STREET, EAST
OMAHA, NEBRASKA. BASED ON IN-
FORMATION THAT THE SUSPECT HAS
LEFT OUR JURISDICTION THE FED-
ERAL BUREAU OF INVESTIGATION
WAS ASKED TO ENTER THE CASE AND
IS NOW COOPERATING IN THIS INVES-
TIGATION.

Swanson promised reporters they could
pose questions after he read the release. But, as

they found out, that didn't mean he planned to answer them.

"What was the motive?" a reporter asked.

"I'm sorry, we can't discuss that," Swanson said.

"Did the suspect know the victims?"

"We can't discuss the relationship between the suspect and any of the victims."

"Has the substance been identified?"

Swanson looked to the other side of the room and nodded to a second reporter.

"Where did he work? Can you tell us anything about Mr. Harper?"

"I'm sorry, we can't."

"What led investigators to believe it wasn't accidental?"

"We can't go into details of the investigation."

The first reporter raised his voice: "What was the substance? What substance was used? We'd like to know."

Swanson tried ignoring the question again, but the reporter insisted. The deputy chief finally said, "We really can't go into that because it might jeopardize the investigation. We can say it's an unusual homicide."

Knowles cut in. Few details were releasable because "the investigation is continuing."

Unable to pry straight answers out of Swanson and Knowles, the half-dozen reporters invaded East Omaha, where they located Steve's residence—empty. Some stumbled onto his parents' home two houses down, but no one came to the door. Instead of running with the pack, an Associated Press reporter phoned the Harper home and obtained the family's only comment. Tearfully, Eva Lou told the writer her son was innocent but authorities were bent on "using his past record against him." Steve's not running away, she insisted, he's out of town on a construction job.

Reporters canvassed the neighborhood, asking the same questions: What type of person was Steve? What were his likes, dislikes? How did he know the victims? Why would he do such a horrible thing? Most people were working and not home. Those who were described Steve similarly: "Never got very personal with anyone"; "a young man who took everything seriously"; "he kept to himself." In their haste to file their stories, reporters passed over the home of the retarded girl and persons who knew of the dump fire accident.

Once back at their desks, the journalists contacted schools, eventually learning Steve had attended North High and Creighton University. Some wondered where the police had obtained a photograph of the suspect to hand out, one resembling a mug shot. Had Steve been arrested before?

After poking at attorneys and parole officers for most of the day, reporters unearthed the sensational link: Sandy and the 1975 shooting. More important, they discovered Steve had once worked at the Eppley Institute. The latter connection contained a public relations nightmare. But institute officials managed to keep the lid on negative headlines by regurgitating what they had fed Detective Miller: Steve "had access to the usual laboratory chemicals, but nothing you would consider fantastically toxic."

The news hounds lost Steve's trail with his resignation at Eppley. So had investigators, and that explained why they graciously held the news conference—to use the media to find Steve.

That night, the television news located the fugitive effortlessly. Moments after Steve's photograph popped up on all three stations, Delores Anderson was on the phone to Channel 3, trying to "get in touch with the proper authorities." The newsroom put her in touch with the Omaha homicide unit, which passed her on to Detective Greg Thompson at home.

Before the end of the newscast, Detective Thompson arrived at Anderson's home on South 50th Street and learned the suspect was working for a company in Beaumont. The woman didn't know the name of the company. Anderson knew Steve's whereabouts, she told Detective Thompson, because her son, Timothy, accompanied Steve to Texas. In fact, her twenty-one-year-old son slept on the top bunk bed of Steve's mobile home.

Tim called home regularly and the night before had told his mother the construction crew planned to pull out the following day for a job in Florida.

Detective Thompson quickly telephoned Sergeant Parker at home. He, in turn, notified the FBI in Omaha, who called the FBI in Texas. Agents in Houston promised to confront Steve the next day.

Early the next morning, Sergeant Parker accepted a long-distance collect call from a man named Dwight Hawbaker, who identified himself as Steve's boss on the Texas project. News traveled fast.

"Steve's at the airport," Hawbaker said. "I think he's buying an airplane ticket to Omaha, but I'm not sure."

After hanging up, the sergeant relayed the information to the local FBI, to pass on to the Houston office. A short time later, Hawbaker called a second time: "I've just talked with Steve. He's buying a ticket to get away."

"Can you find an airport security guard," Sergeant Parker asked, "and bring him to the phone?"

A minute, then two passed without anyone talking on the other end. Maybe Steve was slipping out of the noose. Another minute went by. Sergeant Parker was getting worried.

Suddenly, a breathless Hawbaker came back on the line: "The FBI's just arrested Steve."

Omaha detectives were exuberant over the capture. Without delay, Detective Miller made reservations to fly to Texas.

Book Three

A
MOST
EVIL PLOT

Nineteen

"HOW COULD THIS HAPPEN?" Steve wondered. "It wasn't supposed to be this way!"

Things had been going so well. Now he sat in a dark, dingy cell wearing a white jail jumpsuit; confined, trapped, like the obedient rats he'd kept in his garage. Steve hoped, prayed, he was dreaming. But he wasn't, and he could feel the demons in his mind wanting to return.

If ever confronted by the police, he expected himself to be alert, confident. Instead, he was falling apart. It was imperative that he compose himself to keep the police at bay, off balance. They had no evidence.

The jail cell felt so small, Steve found it hard to breathe, think. At any moment, he might suffocate. He dreaded going back to prison. But, whether he realized it or not, he'd charted that possibility the day he was sentenced for the shooting in 1976. His vengeful plotting began before he left the courtroom back then. And not a day had gone by when he hadn't thought about it while living in the prison's Trusty Dormitory. Steve knew he would get even, he just didn't know when or how.

Pastor Phil Lueck knew it, too: He could tell by the way Steve talked every time they met at the penitentiary. The pastor tried heading off revenge by visiting weekly to read Scripture. For hours, they read the Bible. And on one visit, the clergyman baptized Steve and handed him the book *Adjust or Self-Destruct*. The pastor hoped the Christian book—on humanity coming to grips with sin and the nature of Christ— would guide Steve back to spiritual health. But Steve lived among thieves, rapists, and murderers, a life much more fertile for vengeance than contrition. Besides, Steve's heart was still in a million pieces. He still couldn't comprehend why Sandy Johnson had given him the cold shoulder.

Steve got out of prison a lot sooner than he expected. Those first months out of the pen in the summer of 1977 promised the good life. His faithful friend Pastor Lueck made it a personal challenge to help him adjust, mentally and spiritually, to living outside prison. The pastor weaned him of prison routines, including the habit of letting others make his daily decisions, and accompanied him to church every Wednesday and Sunday. Relatives, too, offered encouragement and a few dollars to help him get a fresh start.

Steve's life blew up, however, when a veterinary school refused to enroll him. It didn't want criminals in its program. His budding confidence plummeted. The rejection seemed to confirm his innermost insecurities, and he didn't even think about applying to other schools.

All he had ever wanted was to be a veterinarian. It was his childhood dream. All the schooling and training—*wasted*. Steve felt worthless, powerless. On hearing the bad news, his mind balked at thinking of anything but rejection. The word went around and around in his mind, like a broken record. The mental stutter lulled him into extreme depression, to the point where he had trouble eating and sleeping.

This latest catastrophe made him want to lash out at Sandy even more, but he hadn't thought of a way to do it without ending up in prison again.

On a few dates with another woman, Steve had fantasized about being with Sandy: her blue eyes, blond hair, and petite figure. Even after he stopped seeing the woman, his mind filled with ideations of Sandy.

Since staying employed was a requirement of his parole, Steve accepted almost any position. He floated from job to job, working as an oiler of heavy equipment for $8.24 an hour; a mechanic's helper for $5 an hour; and a meat cutter boning chuck for $4.65 an hour. All brainless work.

In February 1978, Steve climbed out of his dysfunctional world long enough to visit an employment agency. To his surprise, the agency directed him to the Eppley Institute to apply as a research technologist.

As Steve prepared to start his new job at Eppley in March, Pastor Lueck—his link to both the church and social equilibrium—moved out of East Omaha and into a neighborhood in the far northwest edge of Omaha. Only a few miles separated them, but the distance resulted in the two men losing contact.

With the tie to Lueck broken, Steve stopped going to church. That singular act symbolized his total break from his former life: his family, his dream of becoming a veterinarian, his God. And why not? Neither his family nor God could help him overcome his depression or help him forget Sandy.

Steve saw no loss in trying the sordid side of life, and started frequenting bars, associating with ex-cons he had met in prison. Around his new friends, alcohol appealed to Steve. And when he told his buddies he was having trouble sleeping, over a girl, they supplied Valium and Doriden. The Valium calmed him, the Doriden put him to sleep. Before long, Steve was devouring the addictive drugs in large quantities and washing them down with brandy. Sometimes, he'd go without sleep for a week. Other times, he'd crash for a day or two.

In a final rebellious step, Steve sought out Satan: Perhaps he could help where God had failed. As Christians prepared to celebrate Lent and Jesus' divine exaltation, Steve experienced a transformation that pushed him in the opposite direction. With the help of his new companions, he joined a cult. Convinced he'd turned into an atheist and a humanist, he bought a Satan Bible to delve deep into satanism.

At home nights, Steve mixed brandy, Valium, Doriden, and satanism. What a splendid taste, at least in the beginning. Ultimately, the potent concoction thrust him into the world of black spirits and hallucinations. Once, Satan appeared at his bedside—with throbbing fiery eyes—to terrify him for hours. Steve's perspiration soaked the bed. The spiritual demon forces even brought Steve's mother to him one night, dead.

For weeks at a time, Steve lived on his demonological blend. The moment the brew started wearing off, he'd grab a couple of Doriden pills, mash them up into a powder, and mix them with brandy so his system would absorb them faster.

Nothing mattered anymore.

Eventually, Steve experienced a "crazy splitness" in his thinking. He was turning into two people. At Eppley, he was calm and cool. At home, he was erratic.

Rising above all the dreams and hallucinations was Sandy Johnson. By late summer, the pain of her rejection was unbearable. He felt "blown up inside" all over again. She had made a fool of him. He couldn't get her out of his mind. The more he consumed drugs and brandy to erase her memory, the more he thought of their lost relationship. So vivid was their imaginary intimacy, he often conversed with her. Realizing his folly, he'd sit up in bed and say, "What sort of crazy thing was that?" Sometimes, he'd talk to Sandy all night. One moment he idolized her, for he thought he couldn't live without her. The next, he hated her guts, despised her for ruining his life.

At work, during his longest period of sobriety, Steve toyed with the idea of suicide to end the vicious cycle. He had to do something.

One July day, the solution came to him. Why hadn't he thought of it sooner? Oftentimes, he overheard Eppley researchers talking of a little-understood caustic chemical that was extremely dangerous. Why kill himself? That was stupid. He surreptitiously pocketed a bottle of the exotic stuff.

For several days, Steve left the bottle undisturbed in his home, as if savoring its power to change everything. Off and on, he stared at it, wondering how potent it really was. He decided to find out by pouring some in a bowl of milk in the garage for a family cat. He didn't anticipate his brother's puppy getting into the garage for a drink.

The dog just lay around, but the cat tossed himself about in slow motion like a rodeo bronco trying to buck a cowboy.

The death of the animals surprised Steve. He did not know the chemical was so toxic. For Sandy, he figured he needed but a small amount.

In anticipation of stalking his prey to execute his sick scheme, Steve resigned his job at Eppley in mid-August.

Day and night, Steve shadowed Sandy and Duane Johnson. Several times a day, he'd drive by their home on Fontenelle Boulevard. At night, he'd park on a side street or a parking lot adjacent to their house. The lot was so close to the home, he could see Sandy and Duane inside. Night after night, his jealous eyes followed their silhouettes from the kitchen to their bedroom.

They were as good as dead.

By the end of August, he knew what time the lights came on in the house and when they went off. He knew Duane worked all day and Sandy stayed home with the children. Most of all, he knew the family almost always went out Saturday nights and stayed out late.

Steve was ready. But first, he thought he'd have a little fun. In the early days of September, he telephoned the Johnsons at all hours. When Sandy or Duane answered, he'd hang up.

After about a week of sleepless nights, the Johnsons contacted the phone company, which suggested the installation of a tracing device. However, there was a long waiting list for the limited number of tracers.

Suddenly, the annoying calls stopped. One late afternoon, though, the phone rang at about five.

"Hello?" Sandy said.

"Is Duane there?" a man asked politely.

"He isn't here right now. He went to the store."

"Do you know when he'll be back?"

"In a very short time. Who is calling?"

The phone went dead.

Sandy shuddered. She was sure it was Steve. Her husband doubted it. Even if it was her old flame, Duane pointed out, smiling, there wasn't much they could do about it.

He was right.

Twenty

ON ARRIVING AT THE Jefferson County Airport at 9:30 P.M., Detective K. G. Miller, Detective Greg Thompson, and Deputy County Prosecutor Sam Cooper drove their rented car straight to the Jefferson County Courthouse, where they were ushered into a large basement office while someone went up to the sixth-floor jail to get Steve.

Peeking through the eating tray slot of cell 905 to alert the inmate of visitors, Deputy Merrick J. Brown was taken aback by the bloody mess on the floor. Hurrying inside, he found Steve sitting calmly on his bed, bleeding from both arms. On a wall, scrawled in blood in large letters, was the name SANDY, but the cell was so dark the deputy didn't see it. Deputy Brown yelled for help. A lieutenant ran in, then out to get ice packs for the wounds. For several minutes, the jailers cleaned and bandaged the slashes.

Steve had managed to cut himself by reaching through the bars and breaking a window leading to the outside. He appeared to have lost a lot of blood—his clothes and shoes were covered with it—but the guards thought the scene looked worse than it actually was. Since the wounds didn't appear life-threatening, they escorted the prisoner, in his bloodied jumpsuit, to the waiting arms of the Omaha detectives.

Detective Thompson took charge of Steve in the basement. And after unlocking his handcuffs, the investigator offered him a captain's chair near an open door. Detective Thompson positioned a second chair directly in front of Steve in a way in which the two men's knees almost touched. They sat face-to-face, eyeball to eyeball. So close, they could almost feel each other's breath when they spoke.

The detective hated Steve, but his amicable face and words beckoned the East Omahan to pour his heart out.

"I'm sorry Sandy treated you the way she did," Detective Thompson began. "She shouldn't have done that."

Steve didn't say anything.

"I need to talk to you!"

"Fine," Steve responded without emotion.

"Well, before we talk, do you want to go to the hospital? I see you're cut."

"No," Steve said. He nodded. "I'm fine."

But he wasn't fine: His body shook, visibly, like a coffee cup in the hand of a frail old man. Detective Thompson could see it, but he was there to get a confession.

Before continuing, the investigator read from a Miranda card to ensure that the man in front of him understood that their discussion was serious business, not a Sunday afternoon chat in the park. Steve obviously understood: "I'd talk to you but my attorney said I shouldn't make a statement."

Attorney? How did he get an attorney?

Steve explained that his family had retained Omaha attorney David Herzog, who had instructed him by phone to remain silent. About four that afternoon, he'd been ordered, again, to keep mum, this time by a local lawyer hired by Herzog to handle the case in Texas.

Just then, a jail guard interrupted. There was more blood on the cell floor than originally thought. An ambulance was being summoned to take the inmate to the hospital. Steve attempted to decline medical attention, but the jailer retorted that the choice was not Steve's to make. The jailer said he'd return once the ambulance arrived.

When the interview resumed, Steve still refused to discuss the case without his attorney.

"Just a minute, Steve," Detective Thompson said, stepping outside the office. "I'll be right back."

"We're losing this guy," Detective Thompson told Prosecutor Cooper in the hallway. Detective Miller took notes as the men spoke. "He wants his attorney. He said he would like to tell us about it, but he won't tell us. He wants to rely on his rights."

"I don't give a damn about his rights," Cooper spat impatiently. "I could care less about his rights. I want to know what he used so we can treat the others. I don't want three other people dying. We've got a child who's in bad shape. Do whatever you have to—short of beating him—but find out what he used."

By asking the detective to elicit an illegal confession, Cooper had decided that it was more important to save the lives of the others than convict Steve. The confession was bound to be thrown out. Maybe the entire case.

Detective Thompson didn't argue. Neither did Detective Miller. Detective Thompson walked back into the office, sat down, leaned forward in his seat, stared straight into Steve's eyes, and began talking, nonstop:

"You remember me, don't you? We talked after the shooting a few years ago. Steve, I know you like a brother. I know all about you. I understand how you were in love with Sandy and that she hurt you. I'm sorry she did that to you. I need to talk to you about what happened. Are you going to talk, Steve? You know, your family told us you did it. Yes, *YOUR* family. Your grandmother told us that. It would be better for you if you confessed. Are you going to talk?"

Detective Thompson's words confused Steve. His family would never turn him in. But was it possible his grandmother had said something inadvertently?

"Are you going to talk, Steve? You know, Duane wasn't the only one who died. Chad Shelton, his nephew, also died. Did you know that, Steve? Chad was only eleven months old. He died, Steve. He was a baby, just a baby. Are you going to talk?"

Steve didn't want to remember—he'd tried to block out everything—but the investigator's words were getting to him, making him recall. He wasn't a baby-killer. He had never intended to hurt a child. He didn't care about Duane, but he wasn't a baby-killer.

"You know, Steve, more people might die? Another child might die. Sherrie Johnson might die. Are you going to talk, Steve? Do you want her to die?"

Sick with guilt, Steve shook his head no.

A jail guard poked his head in the room. Detective Thompson ignored him, signaling his desire not to be interrupted. Not now.

"Steve, you need help. You won't go to prison. You'll be put in a mental institution. You can get help there. Are you going to talk, Steve? Are you going to talk? Sandy never should have treated you like that. I'm sorry Sandy did that.

You'll never be electrocuted. I'm here to help you."

"How can you make these promises?" Steve asked. "You're just a policeman."

That was just the sort of question Detective Thompson was waiting to hear, telling him the suspect was cracking, thinking of negotiating.

"I have authority from the prosecutor to talk to you about this. Steve, whatever I decide, goes. I have the authority to deal."

"My attorneys told me not to make a statement," repeated Steve.

Detective Thompson pushed: "Off the record, do you want to tell me what happened? We can't use it against you if we talk off the record. Are you going to talk?"

The phrase "off the record" connected. Steve yearned to get things off his chest, but he didn't want to be held accountable. He could talk now, off the record. It was safe.

"I did it," he blurted out with a big sigh of relief. At the same time, his chin dropped to his chest. "I'm still in love with Sandy. My life has been miserable for the past four years. Everything built up in me. I had to do it."

Steve skipped the nights infested with brandy and the devil, choosing, instead, to lay out the most incriminating steps leading to the deaths.

Looking back up at Detective Thompson, Steve explained that Eppley, whose full name was the Eppley Cancer Research Institute, dealt primarily with chemical carcinogens and their effect on humans. The ultimate objective—as with other cancer research institutes around the country—was to eradicate cancer. Routinely, researchers inoculated animals with a cancer-causing chemical to get cancer growing for experimental purposes. Steve took that idea to heart. His plan was to inoculate Sandy and Duane Johnson with a cancer-causing agent that would kill them years later, when suspicion of murder would be unlikely. He had not intended to kill outright.

As he spoke, Steve occasionally closed his eyes. He saw himself on the night of September 9, quietly walking out of his house and climbing into his pickup truck. He drove west onto Fontenelle Boulevard and slowly passed by the Johnson home. The family car was gone. The lights were out. Good, no one was home. He parked about a block away around a corner. Carefully holding a three-inch-long glass vial, he tiptoed back to the house and found the couple's unlocked bedroom window. Once inside, he felt his way to the kitchen, where he opened the door to the refrigerator just enough to survey the contents. He considered dousing the butter or luncheon meat with the cancer-causing substance, but he figured too much of it would run off. He reached inside the refrigerator and tilted a large white pitcher toward him. Perfect. It contained lemonade. He uncorked his vial and poured the carcinogen in. Noticing the vial still contained traces of the substance, he unscrewed the cap on the milk container and poured the remnants into it. Then, he climbed out the same window and drove off. During the ghastly deed, it never occurred to him that someone other than Sandy or Duane might gulp down the toxin.

Steve still recalled the euphoria of the days that followed. The poisoning was the miraculous panacea he'd been searching for: He stopped drinking, taking drugs, and thinking about Sandy. His obsession vanished. Waking up in the morning was fun again. It was true: Vengeance was sweet.

Steve knew exactly what he had done, but sometimes he was able to detach himself from his demented act. Blank it out. Like the time his mother brought up Duane's death. It caught him by surprise because, in his mind, he was not responsible. Hadn't the media reported that Duane had died of an "infection"? He could have taken a lie-detector test and passed it.

But mothers are not so easily fooled.

By the time Steve left for Texas, he was certain his mother and grandmother suspected him of killing Chad and Duane. He could tell by the way they stared at him—forlornly. It saddened him. He sensed something very personal and precious fading from their relationship.

Like a good homicide investigator, Detective Thompson concealed his emotions lest the killer leave out a detail to keep from offending him. Inside, he was disgustedly incredulous. Sick.

Steve's conniving was far more extensive and revolting—if that was humanly possible—but he didn't go any further. Not until authorities attempted to prosecute him months later would anyone learn the full scope of his demented thinking.

Detective Thompson gently asked Steve to identify the carcinogen—the toxin—to assist the surviving victims.

"D.M.B.A.," Steve mumbled. Truthfully, he didn't quite remember the name of the substance—not that very moment—but he felt compelled to say something. He did not share his uncertainty with his interrogator.

Relieved, Detective Thompson excused himself. In the hallway, he allowed himself to smile as he gave his companions the initials denoting the poison. Cooper cheered. Detective Miller pushed a fist in the air: "I knew you could do it!"

Detective Miller hurried to a hallway telephone and called Sergeant Parker in Omaha, who passed the information on to Douglas County Prosecutor Knowles. He relayed the initials D.M.B.A. to the doctors treating the victims.

Around 11 P.M., Detective Thompson persuaded Steve to sign a consent decree for a search of his mobile home the following day. Shortly thereafter, a medic unit transported the suspect to Baptist Hospital of southeast Texas.

Detective Thompson rode along in case Steve divulged more details. Cooper and Detective Miller followed in the rented car.

At the hospital, a doctor declared the wounds non-life-threatening. By midnight, Steve found himself in a jail cell again, this time shackled to his bed to prevent another suicide attempt.

At a cocktail lounge near their hotel, the three boisterous Omahans toasted their success. Or what they believed to be success.

Book Four
THE SCIENCE MAZE

Twenty-one

SAM COOPER POSSESSED all the attributes that make men successful: good looks, charm, intelligence, schooling at private institutions, a military career, a strong business background, and, above all, a blue-blood upbringing.

At birth on August 8, 1935, in Chicago's Cook County, his chances of ever hobnobbing with the elite looked rather bleak when his natural mother put him up for adoption. No telling where the baby might end up. But he faced wealth instead of despair when Samuel L. and Esther Cooper of Omaha adopted him.

Samuel L. Cooper was a U.S. Navy World War I veteran who owned Cooper & Claypool, a small but profitable Pittsburgh steel company. In the 1920s, he sold it to U.S. Steel so he could move to Omaha and marry Esther Wilhelm, the daughter of Charles Wilhelm, owner of the prominent furniture-manufacturing business Orchard & Wilhelm. Once a member of the Wilhelm family, Samuel L. was recruited to help Esther's father run the family's business, which the old German had established in 1893.

As a child, Sam Cooper—Samuel W. Cooper in socialite circles—lived and played in Gold Coast and Happy Hollow, Omaha's wealthiest neighborhoods. But he turned out to be an asthmatic youngster. To alleviate his medical condition, his parents shipped him off to Fountain Valley, an all-boys private boarding school near Colorado Springs. Summers reunited the family. Frequently, the Coopers spent them on Madeline Island on Lake Superior off the coast of Wisconsin. There, Cooper romped on beaches inhabited by spectacular wild game and ducks.

With ambitions of becoming a career military officer, Cooper enrolled at The Citadel, a prestigious military college in Charleston, South Carolina. After graduating in 1958 with a degree in commerce and the rank of second lieutenant, he joined the U.S. Marines. Just before reporting for duty in Quantico, Virginia, he married his longtime Omaha sweetheart, Angela Donarico. The enormous amount of time spent away from his wife and infant sons proved too much: Cooper resigned his commission in 1962 to return to Omaha and the furniture business. In 1965 his father sold the company, leaving Cooper with more than spare change in his pocket and an opportunity to start a new career. At the age of thirty, the former

Marine chose to become a lawyer and three years later graduated from Creighton Law School.

Cooper quickly discovered that being qualified sometimes had nothing to do with getting a job. On approaching Chief Public Defender Bennet Hornstein for a position on his staff, he was tossed one question: "What political party do you belong to?"

"I'm a Republican," Cooper said proudly.

"If you change your political party, we'll hire you."

"When hell freezes over!" Cooper shot back. He invited Douglas County Prosecutor Donald Knowles for lunch at the Omaha Club, which catered to the rich or powerful. Presto, Cooper was a deputy prosecutor.

Cooper was green, but not a slouch. He worked his share of long hours and with each case he prosecuted it became evident he was meant to be a trial attorney, capable of combining judicial temperament and showmanship with tenacious questioning. Through the years, his ability to work well with irreverent, hard-nosed homicide detectives made him the prosecutor of murderers. Not one to like surprises—especially in high-profile trials—Cooper refused to depend totally on police to prepare a case. He insisted on reconnoitering a murder scene as police came upon it, even at three in the morning. He wanted to get a feel for the crime: the gruesomeness, the stench, the details that would negate or corroborate accounts of the victim's last minutes alive. To keep abreast of the latest tools for investigating sudden deaths, he maintained a special collection of forensic articles and books at home in a large walk-in closet.

Cooper's most obvious trait—one many successful men often lack—was his gentle, unpretentious manner. Few people who associated with him personally or professionally knew of his wealth. Cooper's demeanor attracted respect from those who hovered over both ends of the social and economic scale. Perhaps that explained the peculiar telephone call he received some days after he returned from Texas.

It was early one afternoon when the receptionist at the prosecutor's office dialed Cooper's extension to transfer a call from a man claiming to know about the poisonings. Not only would the caller not give his name, he would speak to no one but Cooper.

"This is Sam Cooper, how can I help you?"

"I'm calling you about the death of Duane Johnson in Omaha," the husky male voice explained.

"Okay," Cooper said, trying to sound relaxed. "Who's calling?"

After a moment, the man responded, "I don't want to tell you. I'm just giving you this information as a citizen. I can't tell you who I am, but you ought to talk to a guy named Bill Trout. He might know about the poisonings."

"Who's Bill Trout?"

"He's a guy who was in prison with Steve Harper. I hear Steve and Bill talked about the poisonings."

"Tell me who you are?"

There was a long pause.

"I don't want to get involved," the man offered. But his next question hit closer at his reluctance to identify himself. "Can I be charged if I knew they talked about this?"

"I'm not going to charge you if you were only aware there was some conversation about the poisoning and you did not participate in a conspiracy."

The prosecutor's explanation persuaded the tipster to disclose his identity. Cooper recognized the name immediately; he was a felon Cooper had sent to prison several years before.

"What goes around, comes around," Cooper thought.

Prosecutors made a lot of informants if they treated criminals evenhandedly, if they refrained from throwing the book at them when they didn't deserve it. Besides, even convicts hated baby-killers.

Cooper had struck pay dirt, provided the caller was telling the truth. There appeared to be no reason for him to lie; he was not after money or leniency on another case. The value of the revelation depended on two things: Trout confirming the conversations and Trout agreeing to testify against an old friend. Neither was a given.

After talking with the informant, an exuberant Cooper excitedly called Detective Miller to share the good news.

Oddly, Omaha investigators already had Bill Trout's name, but they had failed to discover its significance in the murders. During the search of Steve's residence, detectives confiscated a postcard signed B.G.T. The postal stamp indicated B.G.T. was traveling through Nevada. Also, a routine check of the phone calls Steve made after his arrest in Texas revealed one to a Bill Trout.

In scrutinizing Trout's past, Detective Miller easily verified that Trout had met Steve in prison while serving two-to-five years for embezzling more than $19,000 from the Family Service Association in Lincoln, Nebraska. Trout had stolen the money while he was the organization's program director.

The tip rang true. But where was Trout?

His state parole office file indicated he lived in Oakland, California, where he worked as a hardware salesman. He'd left Omaha on September 13, 1978.

"Interesting!" Detective Miller observed. Trout had departed three days after the poisoning. "Was it a coincidence? Or was Trout an accomplice? How many people were involved?"

Cooper and Detective Miller were anxious

to talk with Trout. First, however, they had to extradite Steve from Texas, and one legal maneuver after another was delaying his extradition.

Steve finally lost the legal battle in December, and six days before Christmas Detective Miller and Detective Thompson flew to Texas to return the East Omahan to the Midwest.

Not until January 1, 1979, did Cooper and Detective Miller board a plane to Oakland to ambush Trout, catching him by surprise before he could run or contact Steve. The plan was simple: Have Trout's parole officer ask him to drop by the parole office on January 2 to meet a new "leash."

Trout came in as scheduled. After talking briefly with his parole officer, he was escorted into a back room to meet the "replacement." Instead, he found himself face-to-face with a prosecutor and a large, rough-looking homicide detective.

Detective Miller pulled out a photograph of Steve and shoved it in his face: "Do you know him?"

Nervously, Trout nodded.

The investigator asked about the poisoning.

Trout denied knowing anything. He acknowledged hearing Steve talk about "some very bizarre things" but claimed he couldn't recall any specifics.

Angry, Detective Miller threatened to arrest him, haul him back for a stiff interrogation:

"How would you like to stroll through the airport in handcuffs?"

Cooper interceded. If Trout knew anything, the prosecutor wanted him to open up voluntarily. The last thing he wanted was a hostile witness on the stand.

"Would you be willing to come to Omaha with us to go over this thing in more detail?" the prosecutor inquired in a friendly manner. "It won't cost you anything. We'll pay your airfare, your hotel."

Instinctively, Trout resisted. Even if he'd only met Steve for a beer after they both left prison, Nebraska authorities could revoke his parole for associating with a felon. Yet he felt he needed to do something to appease the prosecutor and this menacing cop. When Cooper offered to sign a note promising he would be allowed to return to California relatively quickly, Trout consented to taking the sojourn.

Over Detective Miller's heated objections, Cooper let the parolee go home. Arresting Trout, in the detective's estimation, was the only way to ensure the son of a bitch got on the plane the following morning.

Surprisingly, Trout showed up. But he was still having trouble remembering his relationship with Steve.

As the three men moved along a narrow passageway in the Los Angeles airport, Detective Miller gave the ex-con his plane ticket. By the time they arrived at their gate five minutes later, Trout had lost it. Cooper and the investigator stared at each other, befuddled. They didn't know what to say or do, at least not in a crowded airport. One thing was sure: They'd been conned by a con man. Just then, a helpful onlooker walked up to Trout, handed him an envelope, and smiled: "Sir, you threw your ticket away. I found it in the trash can."

Twenty-two

PROSECUTOR SAM COOPER couldn't help recalling his own crazy teenage years when he thought of Steve Harper. As an average sixteen-year-old trying to impress the girls, Cooper strutted around like he was God's gift to women. The girls, of course, knew all boys acted like idiots. Harry S Truman ran the White House at the time—making the liberal era of "free sex" light-years away—but dating, whether in the early 1950s or the early 1970s, wasn't much different. Everyone fell in and out of love as often as the bell rang in high school. No big deal.

Steve never got the message, neither from his parents nor from observing the mating game among other teens. Somehow, his mind fixed on Sandy Johnson and within a few months he'd mutated into a monomaniac. Since then, he blamed all his problems on his first and only love. He repeatedly told himself: Because of Sandy everything has gone wrong. If I get rid of Sandy, things will go right.

"Very tragic," thought Cooper, sitting in his office in early January, "but taking murderous revenge was impermissible. It was morally wrong and illegal."

Thinking back on the poisonings to figure out how to proceed with the prosecution, the prosecutor realized that it had been somewhat of a miracle the case had made it this far. If Chad Shelton and Duane Johnson had been taken to different hospitals initially, no one would have linked the deaths, as Nurse Lynda Rummel had. If Dr. R. David Glover had ignored Rummel's observations, there would have been no epidemiological investigation to point to a toxin. If Lieutenant Foster Burchard had waited for medical authorities to come to him, no one would have discovered Steve's heinous solution to a broken heart. No telling how many more girlfriends—and entire families— could have suffered the same fate.

Cooper desperately wanted to convict Steve, get him off the streets forever, but it looked bleak.

The confession was in jeopardy, as he knew it would be, and now it was apparent Steve had lied about using D.M.B.A., whatever that was, as he claimed in Texas. According to the county health department, a Dr. Renate Kimbrough at CDC punched a gaping hole in Steve's contention. She'd fed D.M.B.A. to rats and it took literally pounds of the substance to cause any effect. That eliminated it as the poison, since only a small single dose had killed or sickened the five victims.

Cooper faced other obstacles.

His friend Detective Miller had done admirable work—he'd identified the suspect and had helped put him behind bars—but there was insufficient evidence to guarantee a conviction. It was not Cooper's job to direct investigations, however, and it was imperative that convincing medical evidence be obtained. Specifically, the prosecutor wished to identify the poison. He believed the jury would want to know what had killed Chad and Duane.

Cooper decided to start his own investigation. Technically, he had the authority to gather additional evidence because the case was in the prosecution stage. Unknown to Cooper at the time, his search would turn international, into an area little understood because experimentation on humans is prohibited. By the time the case would reach trial, the prosecutor would log over seventy thousand miles flying around the country.

The homicide files took a terrible beating and several wooden chairs lost their legs when Detective Miller learned that Cooper planned to nose around. The detective believed *HE* was the investigator. It was *HIS* case. If there were loose ends, *HE* should run them down. That's the way the process worked.

"Not on this case," Cooper informed him.

"Are you telling me you don't have confidence in me?"

"No!" Cooper responded. "I'm saying that you're the wrong person for this phase. You're too negative about doctors. They can feel it. Besides, doctors prefer to talk to an attorney rather than a cop."

"Bullshit!" Detective Miller growled. But there was nothing he could do.

The investigator had never been so angry at a friend. Still furious when he got home that day, he told his wife Cooper was trying to take all the glory: "He wants to get me out of the way. He's trying to ace me out. That's not right."

In such a complex case—involving one of the most anomalous murders in history—Cooper was unsure where to begin the hunt for the medical pieces that spelled murder. But he thought the Eppley Cancer Research Institute should be his first stop since Steve insisted that he had stolen the poison from there. Steve's confession in Texas left Eppley officials little room to deny the institute's pivotal role in the slayings.

In the second week of January, Cooper went to see Eppley director Dr. Philippe Shubik, who vowed to help in any way he could. The fifty-seven-year-old European was the first of many foreigners Cooper would meet in a field dominated by physicians from outside America.

Shubik's vitae featured University College at Oxford, University College Hospital Medical School in London, and an internship at London Hospital during World War II. He'd arrived in the United States in 1949 to coordinate cancer research at the Chicago Medical School. He left that position in 1968 to run Eppley at the University of Nebraska College of Medicine.

To begin with, Shubik pointed out, he doubted Steve had poisoned his victims with D.M.B.A., which stood for dimethylbenz(A)-anthracene. Cooper took notes but could not, to save his life, spell the name of the compound. He'd have to get the spelling later. D.M.B.A. was a carcinogen in cigarettes and petroleum products that caused cancer in bone marrow, Shubik explained. Often, pathologists diagnosed radiation as the cause of cancer instead of D.M.B.A. because both precipitated similar changes in the body.

In Shubik's expert opinion, the likely toxin that had killed Chad and Duane was dimethylnitrosamine (D.M.N.), another carcinogen used at Eppley. The postmortem examinations of the boy and his uncle resembled those of laboratory animals given D.M.N. in experiments. D.M.N. was a by-product in the manufacture of rocket fuel, but the anticorrosive agent doubled as a solvent in the rubber industry. In research, scientists used it to induce cancer in animals.

Shubik described the substance as a yellow,

odorless, water-soluble liquid with a sweet taste. Exposure to the chemical resulted in cancer of the liver and kidneys. The compound was also highly toxic. So potent, in fact, gloves were required in handling it to prevent absorption through the skin.

In mice, D.M.N. caused death in two to four days. Animal studies indicated a mere 2.8 grams—or one-tenth of an ounce—could kill a person.

D.M.N. made the perfect murder potion: It metabolized rapidly, meaning most of it disappeared in the body within twenty-four hours. All of it vanished in two days.

Amazing, thought Cooper. No wonder no one was able to detect the poison in the victims, before or after death.

Shubik offered other scientific tidbits about D.M.N. People produced minute amounts of dimethylnitrosamine when they ate certain food products, like fish, ham, baloney, and other luncheon meats. D.M.N. in foods was associated with the use of sodium nitrite as a preservative, which reacted in the human stomach to form carcinogenic nitrosamine. Bacon, on the other hand, created a carcinogenic compound upon being cooked.

Shubik had a confession of his own: Although Steve lacked authorization to experiment with highly toxic carcinogens at Eppley, he had easy access to them. Almost everyone at the institute did.

Cooper was genuinely impressed with Shubik. His comprehensive knowledge of D.M.N. was exactly the type of expertise he sought for the trial. But he couldn't depend on the director as a witness; his testimony could be considered skewed. In the courtroom, conceivably, he might hold back on vital information since it was likely the victims planned to sue the research center.

Shubik recommended that the prosecutor contact a former classmate of his, Dr. Peter N. MaGee, the internationally known director of the Fels Research Institute at Temple Hospital in Philadelphia. The fifty-eight-year-old British subject and another Briton, John M. Barnes, pioneered most of the research into dimethylnitrosamine. From tests on rats, rabbits, mice, guinea pigs, and dogs, the two men demonstrated D.M.N.'s toxicity in 1954. Two years later, they announced that the compound caused liver cancer. Barnes had died some years before, Shubik said, leaving MaGee the world's leading expert.

At the end of the lengthy meeting, the doctor provided his guest with a stack of literature on D.M.N.

"You might want to read this material before you go any further," Shubik suggested.

As Cooper left, half dazed by the science of it all, it became clear his scientific investigation promised to get far more complicated. The area he had drifted into wasn't even easily understood by doctors and specialists. He could see it was going to take scientists to convince a jury Steve was the killer. He, too, would have to become versed in the foggy world of chemical formulas to tell jurors what all the scientific gobbledegook meant. For starters, he had to learn to pronounce the multisyllabic words, tonguetwisters, capable of making him look foolish in the courtroom.

After buying a thick medical dictionary for laymen, Cooper devoted the next few days to studying the medical journals and other material given to him by Shubik.

The most intriguing document turned out to be a report by a special prosecutor in Europe. It was written in German, but Cooper had a university professor translate it into English. Apparently, Steve was not the first person to kill with D.M.N. According to the report, a German chemistry teacher had murdered his wife by putting small doses of D.M.N. in her marmalade.

That riddle began in 1975 with the woman undergoing testing at several medical facilities, where physicians could neither explain nor alleviate her chronic illness. She deteriorated throughout 1976 and began bleeding from the nose and mouth in January 1977. Foul play crossed her mind when her husband continued bringing her marmalade to the hospital. One day, instead of eating it—which would have al-

tered the D.M.N. into an undetectable form—
she asked the hospital staff to test it. Her husband promptly confessed.

The woman died soon after of severe liver
damage associated with D.M.N. poisoning. Fortunately for investigators, she solved her own
murder.

To Cooper, the chemistry teacher's plan was
vile, but Steve's scheme of inducing cancer in
his victims was far more blackhearted.

It astounded Cooper to think that cancer
was the most dreaded disease in modern society, yet civilization manufactured this recognized carcinogen in various forms.

In the hands of the felonious, dimethylnitrosamine truly was the poison of all poisons. It
bothered the prosecutor tremendously that his
unusual murder case could thrust D.M.N.'s potential into the forefront of the criminal world.
He toyed with the possibility of concealing the
identity of the poison from the public. Perhaps
he could persuade a judge to seal all documents
identifying D.M.N. During the trial, both he and
the defense attorney could refer to the poison as
Agent X. The more he thought about it, the
more he dismissed the scheme as unworkable.
The names of many cancer-causing agents were
bound to come up during testimony, not just
D.M.N. He couldn't allude to all of them as
Agent X.

In reality, it was the actual plot—to murder
by cancer—that Cooper wished to keep secret.

But it was too much an integral part of the prosecution. Almost every argument and piece of evidence would be wrapped in the theme.

Besides, a *World-Herald* reporter, Larry King, already had written an article disclosing Steve's intent and the existence of cancer-causing chemicals. He had obtained his information from the court files used to extradite Steve from Texas. Cooper abandoned his hope of secrecy.

Twenty-three

AT MIDNIGHT, SHERRIE JOHNSON awoke crying and pleading for her mother. A nurse at Children's Memorial Hospital calmed the restless girl by giving her toys in bed and letting her walk the halls. Not until 3:35 A.M. did Sherrie, pale with dark circles under her eyes, fall asleep again.

Sandy had admitted her daughter for tests to find out if the poisoning somehow was the cause of constant bruising on the girl's legs and feet. She feared the ugly purple blotches might be a sign of a relapse. The month before, Sallie Shelton had suffered one and found herself in a hospital as weak as on the Sunday she had drunk the spiked lemonade. She looked much worse, though. These days, it was rare for her to go to sleep dry-eyed. She missed her little boy, terribly.

Seeing a doctor gave the surviving victims

some peace of mind, but the short stays in the hospital were rather pointless, medically. Doctors still didn't know what to treat them for. D.M.N. appeared to be the poison, but no one knew for sure.

While doctors at Children's Hospital prepared to perform a liver biopsy on little Sherrie, Sam Cooper packed up his suits and ties in New York City at the conclusion of a forensic-science symposium. Hundreds of sudden-death experts from around the world had attended the conference at the New York City Medical Examiner's Office, but not one had offered Cooper any useful advice on the Omaha case. The poisoning was too exotic.

Instead of returning home, Cooper flew to Philadelphia to drop in on Dr. Peter N. MaGee, the dimethylnitrosamine expert at the Fells Institute, a privately endowed cancer research center at Temple University.

So far, Cooper's repeated attempts to speak with MaGee had failed. Embarrassingly, the veteran prosecutor had been unable to get a call past the secretaries.

"Dr. MaGee is a busy man. He's in a meeting," they told him time and time again.

This time, before leaving Omaha for New York, Cooper simply contacted the Fells Institute to say he was arriving about midmorning that Thursday:

"I've got to have a half hour of his time," Cooper told the secretary emphatically. After putting the prosecutor on hold for what seemed an eternity, the woman came back on the phone.

"The doctor can meet you for lunch on that day." She hung up without waiting for the caller's reaction.

Cooper still expected problems, thinking, "Here comes a guy who wants to mooch a lunch, then bill me a thousand dollars for forty-five minutes of consultation."

Contrary to Cooper's negative expectations, MaGee turned out to be a very pleasant, helpful man. After lunch, he canceled all his afternoon appointments to answer the prosecutor's questions.

In preparing for the trial, Cooper had visited the veterinarian who had tried to save Levi and Cleops. From notes, Cooper proceeded to describe the animals' symptoms to MaGee.

"My God," the doctor said with a gasp, "that's exactly what you get with dimethylnitrosamine. Exactly!"

That was what Cooper had hoped to hear. He believed Shubik, but he preferred to procure the same conclusion from the world's expert to feel sure he'd nailed down the poison. Well, almost nailed down; even MaGee's observations were opinion.

Cooper now sought physical proof. Anything.

There existed no method of detecting D.M.N. in human tissue, but MaGee believed there might be a way to determine whether the compound—known as a methylating agent—passed through an individual's body. A researcher in California was testing animals for telltale signs of D.M.N. exposure. The telltale signs were so minute that measuring them required using "nanomoles" and "picomoles." The researcher's name was Dr. Ronald Shank. He worked out of the University of California outside Los Angeles.

Cooper's eyes lit up. Shank couldn't solve all his problems, but his tests might produce the sole physical evidence of the poison.

After three hours of virtually nonstop questions, Cooper asked MaGee if he'd testify at the upcoming trial. MaGee said he would if paid a consulting fee.

"We can't do that," Cooper advised him disappointedly.

Defense attorneys freely hired expensive experts to take the stand. Prosecutors shied away from the practice out of fear the witnesses would tailor testimony to please the prosecution. And since MaGee was not involved in the investigation, Nebraska could not subpoena him. Cooper asked the doctor to reconsider, but he would not.

After sincerely thanking MaGee for his help, Cooper crammed a stack of notepads into his briefcase and headed for the airport to go home.

* * *

Minutes before boarding his plane, Cooper felt his chest tighten. He was suffering a panic attack. What the hell were methylating agents? What were nanomoles and picomoles? How would he know if Shank's tests were valid? What if Shank's results evaporated under cross-examination by a first-year public defender? The more he thought about science and laboratories and rats and monkeys who were fed mounds of cucumbers three times a day for the sake of research, the more he worried he'd wandered into a scientific tar pit. If *HE* didn't understand it, how did he expect a jury to? Cooper needed help.

He delayed his trip home. He flew to Atlanta, unannounced, to consult Dr. Renate Kimbrough. She was a doctor, a researcher, a toxicologist, and a medical investigator. And she was the only person who had suspected a toxic substance from Eppley from the start. He trusted her, even though he'd never met her or spoken to her.

On the plane, he thought about his friend K. G. Miller. This would set him howling. He was going to feel left out, again.

"I don't understand all this research business," Cooper dejectedly confessed to Kimbrough on arriving at CDC. "Dr. MaGee says the poison was D.M.N., a methylating agent. Do you know what a methylating agent is?"

"Of course I do," she said with a smile. "In fact, I could tell it was a methylating agent when I examined Duane's tissue. I didn't know it was D.M.N., but I told the Omaha Health Department I believed it was a methylating agent from Eppley."

Cooper didn't know it then, but Kimbrough's exposure to cancer research went back to 1958 at New York's Memorial Hospital for Cancer and Allied Diseases. She was no stranger to the personal trauma of the disease, either. As a physicist, her father had conducted research into radiation with no protective clothing and he'd died of cancer at the age of thirty-eight. Her grandparents, too, had died of cancer.

For several days, the prosecutor hung around Kimbrough in her laboratory, peering into microscopes and learning about the pathology of the disease. The two also conducted computer database searches for toxicology information on carcinogens.

Cooper made a lot of headway, but before leaving for Omaha he confided to Kimbrough that he was having doubts about Shank's experiments. Dubious, at best, because they involved animals. Shank had never tried his test on humans.

Sam Cooper stopped in Omaha long enough to direct senior law clerk Marc B. Delman to research the admissibility of scientific experiments as evidence, just in case the defense challenged their use. Then he flew directly to the University of California to introduce himself to Shank, a stocky forty-two-year-old scientist with a lumpy nose. The associate professor of toxicology had earned his Ph.D. from the Massachusetts Institute of Technology.

At the mention of MaGee, Shank volunteered that he'd studied under him for two years at Medical Research Council Laboratories in England. Shank had specialized in chemical carcinogens and the methylation of nucleic acids, primarily DNA (deoxyribonucleic acid), the human genetic building blocks. In his work, he experimented extensively with the chemical carcinogen D.M.N.

Perfect, thought Cooper.

After listening to the prosecutor's predicament, Shank was sure he could help with a series of tests aimed at detecting evidence that a methylating agent had been in a body. In other words, D.M.N. changed a person's DNA by methylating it, tainting it with its methyl properties. The process caused genetic changes, mutations. Shank's tests specifically looked for methylated DNA.

To help Cooper better visualize the methylating process, the professor took a piece of paper and wrote out the chemistry name for D.M.N.:

$$CH_3$$
$$\backslash$$
$$N - N = O$$
$$/$$
$$CH_3$$

In the body, the CH_3 reacted with DNA to form methylated DNA. Tissue from the victims was required to conduct the tests.

"What would it cost to do the tests?" Cooper asked.

"It wouldn't cost you anything," Shank said. He grinned. "I'd welcome the opportunity to perform the analysis on human tissue."

Cooper now understood the general methylating concept and leaned toward asking the professor to run the tests, but he wanted to comprehend the chemistry and biology involved. He also wished to find out how good a witness Shank might be.

Could the professor please explain the actual interaction and changes in the body?

"Certainly!"

Shank started scribbling formulas on a blackboard on the left side of a classroom. By the end of the day, the formulas and diagrams spanned the entire width of the classroom on several blackboards.

Sheepishly, Cooper admitted he'd missed a turn or two. Shank had planned to go boating the following day but canceled the outing to re-turn to the blackboard in the hopes of making a difference in the trial.

Cooper liked his patience.

Twenty-four

LAWRENCE J. CORRIGAN joined the Douglas County Public Defender's Office just in time to defend Steve Harper, whose case tumbled into the public coffers when his family realized it couldn't afford a private attorney for a long, drawn-out murder defense. Although Corrigan was the new kid on the block, he was not a novice to the profession. For more than fifteen years he'd practiced law, including four years as a prosecutor. That made him a rare bird; public defenders usually became prosecutors instead of the other way around. Corrigan departed the prosecutor's office for private practice in 1970, just as Sam Cooper arrived to spar for the first time in the legal arena. While the Douglas County District Court docket billed the bizarre murders as "State of Nebraska vs. Steven Harper," the battle in the courtroom translated into Corrigan vs. Cooper: two Chicago-born

Creighton Law School graduates who'd earned
their spurs in the prosecutor's office.

Corrigan was a tall, thin man with dark,
bushy eyebrows and sideburns who walked
with his head tilted to one side and chin slightly
tucked in. He already knew the Harpers. As a
young attorney, he'd helped Jesse Harper with
the legal aspects of setting up a boys' football
team. Now the chief deputy public defender
was dealing with the family on far more serious
matters.

On his first visit to the county jail, Corrigan
was grateful to meet a cooperative, soft-spoken
client instead of the usual scar-faced convict eager to accuse police of a frame-up. Steve readily
admitted poisoning the families. But, like most
criminals, he didn't want to go to prison. The
law obligated Corrigan to represent his client to
the best of his ability, to the point of getting
him off. And naturally, Corrigan intended to
enter a plea of not guilty.

It was never easy persuading a jury to ac-
quit a guilty man, but the chances looked good
for Steve. In Corrigan's mind, his client could
depend on two solid advantages:

- The murders were highly unusual. If jurors viewed them as inconceivable, un-
  thinkable, they would have trouble convicting anyone of murder.
- The evidence was circumstantial. No one
  could directly connect Steve to the
  deaths.

If the prosecution appeared to be developing a stronger case, the most obvious strategy dictated that Steve claim he was insane, which would at least save him from the death penalty. The insanity defense seemed particularly viable in light of Steve's suicide attempt in Texas. Since his arrival in Omaha, guards monitored his cell twenty-four hours a day. He was also under the care of a county psychiatrist who was treating him for "reactive depression" with a combination of psychotherapy and antidepressant medication.

In the early months of 1979, Corrigan sought out numerous psychiatrists to test the insanity defense. For a while, Steve was spending more time talking to mental health specialists than jailers. Of the experts Corrigan contacted, the most reputable was Dr. James F. Gilligan, director of the Institute of Law and Psychiatry at McLean Hospital in Belmont, Massachusetts. Gilligan also served as director of Bridgewater State Hospital, the maximum-security facility for the criminally insane. Gilligan flew to the Midwest to interview Steve, who gladly chronicled his tragic life: his humble East Omaha roots, strong Christian upbringing, the painful dump fire, his dreams of becoming a vet, the degrading courtship with Sandy Johnson, the shotgun attack, and, finally, the poisoning. He even revealed his visit to the hypnotist in Oklahoma.

In the end, Gilligan declared Steve sane,

concluding the murders involved too much planning for him not to know the consequences of his actions.

In debriefing Gilligan and his other consultants, Corrigan explored the possibility of allowing Steve to testify on his own behalf. His sob story might elicit sympathy from the jury. Don't do it, he was warned; it would be a grave mistake. The psychiatrists believed Steve harbored such a strong sense of guilt that what he agreed to say before he took the stand would most probably become something different during the trial, seriously damaging chances of an acquittal.

Corrigan was left with no choice but to abandon the not-guilty-by-reason-of-insanity defense. Still, he asked Gilligan for a written report—just in case—but instructed him to leave out anything that would involve any admissions by Steve.

Like Prosecutor Sam Cooper, the more Corrigan tried to understand the mechanics of how Chad Shelton and Duane Johnson had died, the more exasperated he became. After several weeks on the case, he had to admit he was wallowing in hard-to-discern medical records and literature on carcinogens. He needed help. Corrigan turned to John McGuire, a local chemist who worked for a group of Omaha doctors. McGuire gave Corrigan a crash course in chemistry and obtained articles and textbooks germane to the anticipated toxicological testimony. But both men knew journals and books, no matter how weighty, didn't win acquittals. Oral testimony from experts did. After compiling a list of several prospects, the defense attorney and his adviser flew to Detroit to interview a few. In every field there were two kinds of experts: the known and the unknown. Corrigan demanded the former, a nationally recognized individual whose name and credentials alone stood for unquestionable truth. Before departing Detroit, he'd hired the services of Wayne County Chief Medical Examiner Dr. Werner U. Spitz, one of the world's foremost authorities on violent death and the coeditor of *Medicolegal Investigation of Death: Guidelines for the Application of Pathology to Crime Investigation*. It was a rare homicide detective who had never used the book on an investigation. As a private consultant, the German-born doctor had participated in some of the United States' most notorious deaths: the assassination of President John F. Kennedy, the murder of civil-rights leader Dr. Martin Luther King, Jr., and the drowning of Mary Jo Kopechne at Chappaquiddick.

In the months to come, Spitz would examine all medical records with an eye toward making sure Omaha authorities reached the correct conclusions. Independently, he would ascertain that Chad and Duane had died from a poisonous substance. It would be Spitz's opinion, however, that the deadly poison could have been a number of compounds: D.M.N. or one of *SEVERAL* other methylating agents. In his view, no one could say, absolutely, D.M.N. *HAD* to be the poison. Corrigan considered Spitz's analysis invaluable since Cooper insisted on proving D.M.N. killed the victims. If the prosecutor failed, thought the public defender, the jury might doubt other testimony, leaving the door open for a finding of not guilty.

As summer approached, the defense focused on getting the confession thrown out: It seemed to be the prosecution's only incriminating evidence. Corrigan traveled to Texas to depose the jailers, hospital staff, and the Beaumont attorney who had advised the defendant to remain silent. By the end of June, Corrigan asked for a pretrial hearing to argue against the use of his client's statements. He also arranged for the hearing to handle a request from the prosecution.

If nothing else, pretrial hearings served as a stage for judicial deals: big and small, fair and unfair.

In this case, Cooper sought a deal to help Sherrie Johnson and Sallie and Bruce Shelton. They showed no signs of improving. The attending physicians thought it might help knowing—from Steve, the only one who really knew—the name of the poison, the amount used, and whether it was mixed with other chemicals. If

Steve divulged the information, the prosecutor swore, his role in identifying the substance would not be used as testimony against him during the trial.

To ensure the prosecutor's overture was not a trick, Corrigan discussed the offer with Douglas County District Judge James Murphy, who was to preside over the trial. In giving the arrangement his blessing, Judge Murphy told the public defender he would take any compassionate disclosures into consideration at sentencing if Steve was convicted.

Steve didn't think he had a choice: He was boxed in. It seemed to him the judge would also consider his reluctance at sentencing if he refused to come forward. Thought Steve: "It could do nothing but help me."

In an instant, Steve could have picked up a phone in the jail and given the information to the doctors. The sooner they knew, the better for the victims. Instead, he and his attorney decided to make the revelations on the record, during the pretrial hearing. If Steve provided the valuable data informally and was convicted, Corrigan thought, he "would not get any credit for making the disclosures from subsequent judges" during any appeal process. To cover all their legal bases, the two men also agreed to let Corrigan, rather than Steve, furnish the name of the substance and dosage.

On the morning of July 2, 1979, Corrigan, Steve, Cooper, and a court reporter gathered in

Judge Murphy's courtroom for the pretrial hearing. As prearranged, they closed it to the public. Journalists squawked and whined, but there was nothing they could do.

After homicide Detective Greg Thompson and Detective K. G. Miller testified at length about their role in the Texas confession, a somewhat wobbly Steve took the stand. Corrigan began the questioning by inquiring about Steve's encounter with Detective Thompson:

"How were you feeling at the time that you first got down into that room?"

"I was feeling terrible. I was certainly nauseous to my stomach. The best way I can explain it is that I just felt like I was a third person watching myself. I felt detached from reality."

"Did you have any feeling in your head?"

"Yeah, I wasn't thinking, or nothing was functioning through my head . . . it was spinning over the—the immediate events that just happened. It was certainly total confusion."

"Did you ask him to go to the hospital?"

"No, I don't remember asking him to go to the hospital."

"What do you remember about the conversation? What did you say during the course of the conversation?"

"I told him I would remain silent and I wanted an attorney present."

"Did he then stop his interrogation?"

"No, he kept on talking."

"What'd he say?"

"He just continually talked about it would be best for me if I'd tell him anything he wants to know and . . ."

"Did he say anything about having a lawyer?"

"I continually repeated to him more than a dozen times that I had nothing to say and I wanted my attorney present. And he told me an attorney wouldn't do no good, that it would be best to talk to him. He also told me that he thought I was sick mentally, because he mentioned quite a bit about going to a mental institute."

"A mental institution rather than being prosecuted?"

"Yeah, I assume."

"Do you remember having any conversation about going off the record?"

"I continually told him, the best I remember, that I had nothing to say and I wanted my attorney present. And he told me that 'we'll talk off the record.'"

It was Cooper's turn to question the defendant. Contempt filled his voice.

"Do you recall making the statement to Officer Thompson that you were still in love with Sandra Johnson and everything built up in you and came to a point?"

"I don't understand what you mean by built up, come to a point."

"Did you make a statement to that effect to Officer Thompson?"

"I don't remember anything about built up, come to a point. I believe I told him—or he asked me about my affection towards her, and I told him that I had loved her."

"Officer Thompson testified this morning to the effect that you had made admissions to him concerning going into the Johnson residence . . . that your cat, your dog had been killed as a result of drugs that you'd taken from Eppley. He testified that you told him that you used a drug by the name of D.M.B.A., that you took it in a vial and poured it in milk and lemonade. Do you recall making those statements to Officer Thompson?"

Corrigan interjected: "What he's attempting to do here is improper, Your Honor. I think that the witness ought to be . . ."

"Well, the question calls for a yes or no answer," Judge Murphy said. "Can you remember it, or can't you remember it . . . making those statements to Officer Thompson?"

"Your Honor, I can't say that I made statements," Steve responded, "because Officer Thompson, for the most part, as I remember, told me what I did."

"You don't remember making these statements, then?" Judge Murphy asked. "I take it your answer is no?"

"No," Steve said, "I can't say that I made these statements."

"Are you saying that Officer Thompson

made those statements to you?" Cooper pushed loudly, incredulous.

"Yeah . . ."

"May I have a continuing objection to this, Your Honor?" Corrigan asked.

"You may," said the judge with a nod.

Cooper settled down, then continued: "Officer Thompson told you that there were three people who might be affected by this drug. Do you recall him saying that to you: three living people?"

"Yes . . . I remember Officer Thompson telling me about the health and welfare of other people that might be affected, yes."

"Okay," Cooper said. "After he told you that, were you at all concerned about those other people?"

"Well, yeah, I—I don't remember what I said, but certainly I was. I didn't want anybody else, or wouldn't want to see anybody else, um, get more sick or—or die or whatever."

"All right. And because of that, was your attitude one that you would provide information to Officer Thompson, if you could, that might be of assistance to him?"

Corrigan interrupted again: "May I have a continuing objection to this?"

"You do," the judge stated with a touch of impatience. "The same ruling."

"Your Honor," the public defender finally said, "at this time I'm going to invoke the Fifth

Amendment, and I'm going to counsel my client not to answer that question."

"I think he has answered it," Cooper snickered. "I have no more questions at this time."

It was obvious Steve had confessed, but it was just as obvious his Miranda rights had been blatantly violated. At the end of the day-long hearing, Judge Murphy ruled the confession inadmissible. The judge made it clear, though, that the prosecutor could use it if the defendant took the stand during the trial to deny the poisoning.

Before everyone left the courtroom, the defense kept its end of the bargain: Corrigan identified the poison as D.M.N. (dimethylnitrosamine) and claimed his client had used only six to seven milliliters. Slightly over a teaspoon.

Twenty-five

DR. RENATE KIMBROUGH's supervisors had grown tired of seeing her labor on the Omaha poisonings, but their displeasure did not become apparent until she received a letter from Sam Cooper. In his easygoing manner, the prosecutor praised her diligence and dedication and asked whether she would testify in the upcoming murder trial of Steven Roy Harper.

Of course, she thought, smiling to herself. In a minute! She was having the time of her life sleuthing for murder evidence. Being a part of such a significant medical hunt excited her, and now the payoff: to be out front in the case, in the courtroom, instead of sitting in the background, in the laboratory, as usual.

Her exuberance disappeared the second she handed the letter to her supervisor. He frowned.

"I don't know," he said, shaking his head. "That's going to get us in trouble."

Trouble? What kind of trouble?

The emphasis at the Centers for Disease Control is on diseases, not homicides, he explained. CDC did not want to drift into the "homicide business." She would be setting a bad precedent by testifying.

"Oddball," Kimbrough muttered under her breath. "What idiotic thinking."

In mid-August, Kimbrough mailed the prosecutor a short note explaining CDC's position: "In response to your letter of June 22, 1979, I have finally determined that the Centers for Disease Control does not like to have its employees testify in court cases."

But moments after dropping the envelope in the mailbox, Kimbrough vowed to ignore her boss's asinine attitude: Convicting a killer was far more important than laboratory politics. Besides, she had promised Cooper she'd help him navigate the science maze.

About the time the correspondence arrived at the Douglas County Prosecutor's Office, Kimbrough and Cooper were busy exchanging phone calls and making final preparations to test Shank's premise.

On August 20, a Monday, the prosecutor flew to Atlanta to rendezvous with Kimbrough. She had devised a perfect way of validating Shank's experiments to detect a methylating agent in human tissue: a "blind test." Under the

scheme, tissue from the Omaha victims and un-
related cases from around the country would be
given to Shank to inspect for methylated DNA.
Each sample would be identified by a number,
not the name of the case or the victim. Kimbrough and Cooper would be the only ones who
would know which samples belonged to the
Omaha poisonings.

Cooper was jubilant, but there remained a
major problem: Omaha pathologists had failed
to save enough tissue from the victims. Moreover, CDC possessed only stained tissue from
Chad, rendering it useless for further testing.
Kimbrough and Cooper had no choice but to
try the blind test with only minuscule specimens from Duane.

On August 21, Shank flew to Atlanta. At the
airport, Kimbrough and Cooper handed him a
large Styrofoam box containing eight tissue
samples frozen in dry ice. They were labeled
Tox. No: 23675 Kidney; 23677 Liver; 23851
Liver; 23853 Kidney; 23854 Liver; 26689 Liver;
26690 Liver; 26691 Kidney. Since Steve's trial
wasn't far away, Shank immediately boarded
another plane and flew back to his University of
California lab. The next morning, he and his senior graduate student would begin the analysis.

Twenty-six

It would have been easy for Pastor Philip Lueck to give up on Steve Harper. Who could blame the minister for shaking his head in disbelief, disgust, and walking away, refusing to have anything to do with the East Omahan? But the pastor wasn't repulsed. Instead, he was drawn closer to the young man by his latest predicament. Lueck demanded only one thing in exchange for his unending support: complete honesty. And that explained his first words on visiting Steve for the first time in the Douglas County jail: "Did you do it? Did you poison those families?" Without hesitating, Steve respectfully answered, "Yes." At once, the clergyman set out to tear Steve away from demonology and guide him back to faith in God. Several times a week, he stole time from teaching, grading papers, and his family to drop by the jail to evangelize Steve.

As the trial approached, the pastor detested what he saw and heard during his comings and goings from the jail. In his view, the legal maneuvering was just a deceitful plot to get Steve off, which served only to encourage his dishonesty and criminal denial.

"What good did that do for Steve as a person? As a Christian?" he thought.

In his growing role as his friend's spiritual counselor, Lueck took it upon himself to dissuade Steve from pleading not guilty.

"You have to start being honest with yourself and others and not try to manipulate the system and get out of this," he told Steve sternly during one visit. "Put your trust in the Lord. Be honest, say you're sorry, and accept the punishment."

Steve stuttered that he wanted to be totally open but was afraid to get the death penalty. He feared being electrocuted.

"God doesn't always step in. God doesn't always untie the knots we put into our spiritual shoelaces," the clergyman preached. "Often, he lets us live with the consequences. Just try God."

Steve didn't know what to do, especially when the demons reasserted themselves, talking crazy things to him. Four tempestuous entities pulled his mind in opposite directions: God and his spiritual representative yanked one way, while Satan and his secular comrade tugged the other.

"I felt ready to crack," he later said. "I was afraid I was going to lose my mind. It was so dark in the cell. I was getting so that I didn't know if I was dreaming things or things were really happening. I would wake up and think my mother was calling me."

The merciless storm in his mind became too fierce to handle in the days just before the start of the trial in mid-September. As the voice of God and the biblical passages of Pastor Lueck brawled with the icons of Satan and the legalese of defense attorney Corrigan, Steve's mind snapped. He grabbed a razor blade and cut his wrists. Then he took the metal edge of a toothpaste tube and cut some more.

The suicide attempts landed him in the hospital, where psychiatrists again tried diagnosing his problem. After a day or so, Steve was put on Thorazine, a powerful antipsychotic drug, and placed in a special jail cell.

For Prosecutor Cooper, the prisoner's gestures meant little else than attempts to be found incompetent to stand trial.

"Steve was playing games the last month before trial," Cooper said. "I think he was trying to raise questions about his mental capacity."

Sincere or not, the suicide attempts devastated the Harpers, who regularly saw their son in jail. In between visits, the inmate used his allotment of ten dimes a week to call home.

"I can hardly talk to him without bawling," Jesse Harper admitted to a visitor to his home one day. "He's tried to kill himself three times, but I can't bring myself to talk to him about it."

Twenty-seven

STEVE HARPER SAT MOTIONLESS, glancing neither left at the jury box nor right at the large jail guard standing adjacent to the oversized door leading from the courtroom to the judge's chamber. Back straight and hands folded together on his lap, he gave no hint of the demonic storm roaring in his mind.

When arrested, thick sideburns and a mustache accented bushy reddish-brown hair growing down to his nape, where it curled slightly at the outside edges to create the appearance of two small horns protruding from his neck. To sway the jurors, he shaved off the mustache and cut his hair and sideburns short, like a college student interviewing for his first job. His clothes painted a less favorable picture. He wore a green silk long-sleeved shirt with beltless brown pants.

While Steve pretended to be oblivious to his surroundings that Tuesday morning, the courtroom slowly filled with reporters and a mixture of courthouse employees and curious citizens. In the gallery, directly behind Steve, sat his mother, Eva Lou, emotionally drained but dry-eyed. Each day of the trial she would arrive early to sit as close as she could to her son.

Surveying the twelve jurors—five women and seven men selected the previous day from a pool of sixty jittery people—Prosecutor Sam Cooper still worried over the complexity of the medical and scientific evidence. A year before, he'd never heard of platelets and dimethylnitrosamine. He hoped Steve's peers paid close attention.

Something else nagged at him. He feared the defense would play up, hammer at, the relationship between Steve and Sandy to confuse the jury, prompt them to wonder whether "Mrs. Johnson" wanted out of her marriage. Eventually, the jurors might wonder: Who really spiked the lemonade? Did Steve give the poison to Sandy to use? Why didn't Sandy get sick? Whether anything was going on between Steve and Sandy at the time of the poisoning was immaterial for the purposes of winning a verdict of innocent.

Cooper rose from his chair and walked toward the jury box with a single white sheet of paper in his right hand. He was familiar with every twist and turn of the case, but he'd made a brief outline to remind himself of the main points to make in his opening statement. It said:

Motive
Odd Poison
2??s
Shooting
Scientists
DMN-Metabolizes
Trout

After studying the outline one last time, he looked up at the jurors:

"What I say at this point is not evidence. What Mr. Corrigan says at this point is not evidence. It's simply an opportunity to tell you what evidence we intend to present and how we intend to prove our case.

"You know the charge in this case is two counts of murder and three counts of poisoning. I want to caution you that the state is not required, in this case or in any other case, to prove motive. I think, when you've heard all the evidence, the motive will be very clear in your minds. But the state does not have the burden of proving it.

"We talk of poisons. Before this case came up, I thought of poison in terms of arsenic or strychnine, that kind of thing. We're only required to show the substance was such that it acted to destroy or maim or alter the bodily processes or functions of the victims. The state does not have to prove what compound was used in this case. But, again, I think the state will do that and I think you'll know what was used and how it was done.

"And the issues are really going to boil down to two things: One, was this the result of poison? Were these two deaths and these three illnesses the result of poisonings? And two, was Steven Roy Harper responsible?"

Cooper described Steve's chaotic relationship with Sandy and detailed the shooting in 1975. Using a family tree chart on an easel, he introduced the jurors to the extended family, carefully explaining who had dropped by the Johnson household the day of the poisoning. He summarized the evidence, pointing to lemonade as the vehicle for the poison, the police department's hunt for Steve, and how the medical investigation dead-ended:

"Scientists and researchers had to be brought in. They determined the poison was a carcinogenic compound named dimethylnitrosamine."

The word rolled out perfectly.

"I'm going to talk to you about dimethylnitrosamine, a drug which metabolizes in the body so that upon autopsy or after it's been ingested you're not going to find it in a chemical form. You're going to find segments of it broken down in the body. It was discovered in the 1940s. No one has ever given a human being a great big dose of this stuff to see what happened. The victims in this case bled internally, everywhere."

Cooper paused and gestured toward Steve.

"You're going to hear from a man named Bill Trout. Mr. Trout was a friend of Mr. Harper and they had some conversations concerning what happened. I think I'd best leave that conversation for Mr. Trout to tell you about.

"I think—when all is said and done here, at the end of two and a half or three weeks, however long it takes—that you'll have a very clear picture of what occurred, how it occurred, why it occurred. And you'll have a clear picture of Mr. Harper's guilt on all five counts.

"I can do no more than to ask you to live up to your oath and to be objective and to be fair to everybody and listen very carefully to the evidence. Much of the evidence in the case will be circumstantial, but the prosecution will prove its case nonetheless."

Defense Attorney Lawrence Corrigan waited for Cooper to sit down before approaching the jurors. He spoke deliberately slow, but in a loud voice:

"This case involves three sisters: Sallie Shelton, Sandra Johnson, and Susan Conley. The biggest problem you will have in this case is the cause of the deaths. There is talk about dimethylnitrosamine. But it is a substance which is present in a lot of things: peanut oil, bacon. It's not exactly a secret or an unknown.

It's in almost everyone's system. The theory of the state is that Mr. Harper got the substance from the laboratory he worked at. But it can be ordered from drug companies by any laboratory.

"The state's witnesses will include some of the best testers in the world. When you start with the answer, you'll be surprised how many times you're right. In fact, Mr. Harper had nothing to do with the dimethylnitrosamine area of research, but it sells well as far as the theory goes. Duane Johnson was a truck driver who dealt with anhydrous ammonia.

"There are many, many areas in this case without answers. The issue in this case is that the cause of these deaths must be proven beyond any reasonable doubt. You may find at the end of the state's case that there will be no need to put a defense on."

Before returning to the defense table to join his client, Corrigan shrugged his shoulders in disappointment: "Mr. Harper will not take the stand. I hope you will not hold that against him. That is just one of the difficult decisions I must make as his attorney."

For the first time, the public was about to experience—through the words, gestures, and grief-stricken faces of the trial participants—every messy detail of the heinous plot.

Cooper chose to begin the state's case with the motive: Sandy Johnson. Over her blue eyes, blond hair, petite, shapely figure, Steve had killed. Over a woman! It was the oldest motive in the world.

By now, the prosecutor understood why Detective K. G. Miller despised Sandy. It was Cooper's practice to interview each witness before trial to go over their testimony. When he tried contacting Sandy, he couldn't find her. She'd disappeared. Concerned, he called the Bettens and the Beards. They hadn't seen her in weeks. He called the Sheltons. Sallie and Bruce hadn't heard from her either. Before hanging up, Bruce observed: "It's a funny thing. Sandra's shown no grief for her husband."

When Sandy ultimately surfaced in a small town north of Omaha, she was aloof about everything, even the trial.

"She didn't strike me as the normal bereaved widow," Cooper would say later. "I didn't see a great deal of emotion."

In fact, Sandy had remarried five months after Duane's death. Generally, Jean didn't meddle in her children's affairs, but the new husband joined the family so unexpectedly she felt compelled to probe.

"He came out of nowhere. I wanted to know who he was," Jean explained after the trial. "We were talking on the phone and I asked her how she came to meet him."

"I went to a dating service," Sandy answered. "It matched me up with Bruce."

"That cost money, didn't it?"

"Yeah, it cost me five hundred dollars."

"Boy, did you get robbed," Jean said with a laugh. "Oh my God! Couldn't you go to a bar, go to a dance or something?"

"Well, you don't know what you can find at a bar," Sandy replied seriously.

Cooper had counted on introducing a grieving widow as his first witness, not a new bride. He was shocked to learn of the marriage, just as he was taken aback by Sandy's feelings about Steve: "The only thing he knew how to love were animals."

Now, as Cooper walked out into the hallway to ask Sandy to kick off the prosecution, he sensed "she wanted to get in the courtroom, give her testimony, and get the hell out of there."

Since witnesses are required to provide their names before testifying, Sandy's marriage wasn't a secret very long. Eyeballs rolled in the gallery. Her former lover remained expressionless.

Asked her new married name, she requested that she not be forced to give it out in public. Cooper obliged and referred to her as Mrs. Johnson.

Sandy displayed little emotion during a day and a half of testimony. Not until she recounted her husband's last days did she break down and cry: "Sherrie and Duane were talking, but they were lifeless. His eyes were all full of blood. Duane had big blots of blood all over his eyes."

Cooper appreciated the tears, although he

wasn't sure they were real. After a short recess to let Sandy compose herself, Cooper asked the witness if there was any person in the world, other than Steve, who had a motive to harm her family.

"No," Sandy said without hesitating.

Crocodile tears. That's what Corrigan seemed to think of Sandy's emotional release, and he intended to dwell on her remarriage a bit before moving on to more substantial areas.

"May I ask you how old you are?" Corrigan asked.

"I'm twenty-six."

"What's your date of birth?"

"Eleven–twenty-seven–fifty-two."

"What's your name now?"

Cooper cut in to protect his witness: "I'd object to that, Your Honor."

"The objection's overruled," Judge James Murphy said.

"Sandra Marchant," she said coldly.

"And how do you spell that?" Corrigan asked.

"M-A-R-C-H-A-N-T."

"And your husband's name?"

"Bruce."

"You and Bruce were married when?"

"February 20, 1979."

Doubt. Every chance he got, the defense attorney planned to inject a twist of doubt. His client could not be found guilty if a reasonable doubt existed, especially as to the cause of death. And red herrings? Corrigan thought of plenty. With Sandy, he inquired, "Do you know if he [Duane] was using turpentine around the house?" "Can you tell me: Did that air conditioner come with the house when you bought it from Thomas Realty?" "Where did you buy the paint for the house? Did anyone check the paint?" "What sort of chemicals did Duane Johnson haul in his trucking job?"

Corrigan even tried suggesting that the water at the Johnson home might be the root of the ordeal.

Bruce Shelton took the stand next. And after he testified for the prosecution, Corrigan's doubt campaign continued: "You shampooed your rug that Sunday. Were you using any particular soap?" "Has anybody ever come over to your house to ask to see the soap?" "What was wrong with the tacos?" "Why were they thrown out?"

For three and a half days, Cooper called members of the extended family into the courtroom: Daniel Betten, Jean Beard, Susan Conley, Elaine Betten, Harold Betten, Sallie Shelton. Eyes still blank with grief, Sallie looked as if she would collapse any minute.

Each contributed a piece to the depressing chronology, which was intended to send the jurors home every night with visions of death tumbling in their heads.

At the end of the week, the prosecutor shifted away from the victims and summoned health department director Dr. Warren J. Jacobson and epidemiologist John Wiley to dispel any notion an infectious disease had caused the deaths.

Twenty-eight

BILL TROUT HEDGED, parried, and feigned ignorance. He even obtained an attorney to keep
Omaha officials at bay. But nothing worked.
Eventually, he divulged Steve Harper's secret. If
he had continued to balk, the prosecutor would
have revoked his parole for associating with
felons, meaning a trip back to prison. Knowing
it was Steve's skin or his, he appeared as scheduled at the Douglas County–Omaha Hall of Justice on Monday morning at the start of the second week of the trial.

Trout's narrative of what Steve had contemplated doing with dimethylnitrosamine was going to shock the senses of every individual in
the courtroom and the city. But first, Cooper
needed to expose Trout's criminal past to dull
and preempt the use of such information by the
defense to discredit the witness.

"Okay. Have you ever been convicted of a
felony?"

"I have."

"And when was that?"

"In 1976."

"And what were you charged with?"

"Embezzlement."

"And would you tell us what, in fact, you did?"

"I took money from the Lincoln-Lancaster Child Care Center program in Lincoln. It's a part of Family Service in Lincoln."

"And did you eventually enter a plea, or were you found guilty?"

"No, I entered a plea of guilty."

"Where had you been employed before then?"

"At the Nebraska Department of Education."

"And did you at any time misrepresent yourself to the Nebraska Department of Education?"

"I claimed to them that I had a master's degree in education administration, which I did not possess."

"What is your educational background?"

"Altogether, I have probably three and a half years of college."

"And where were you employed before that?"

"In Gering, Nebraska, public schools."

"For how long?"

"Umm, ten years."

"And in what capacity?"

"As a teacher and as an administrator."

"And where were you employed before that?"

"At my father's firm in Mitchell, Nebraska."

"What kind of firm is that?"

"It was a manufacturing company."

"How long did you work there?"

"About three years, a little over three years."

"Why did you leave?"

"Umm, I had taken some money from his business."

"Were you ever charged with anything in that case?"

"No, I was not."

With Trout's unsavory side out of the way, Cooper maneuvered the witness into a position to recount several intimate conversations with Steve.

Without a trace of contrition in his voice, the ex-con began chronicling his relationship with Steve by telling the jury he had met the defendant in prison while serving time for embezzlement. Even though Trout was almost twenty years older than Steve, the inmates found common ground in their extensive education, something most criminals lack. After becoming friends, Trout and Steve did everything together. Often, Steve expressed bitterness over losing his girlfriend and on several occasions vowed to kill her.

" 'I'm going to get Sandy when I get out! She's going to pay!' " Trout quoted Steve as saying. "If he couldn't have her, nobody could have her."

The men's brief friendship ended in 1977 when Steve left prison.

Trout got out in May 1978. But even then, the state required him to live at an Omaha work release center for several months. During the day, he worked at the Midlands Information and Referral Agency, an organization geared to helping people deal with alcoholism and other family crises. His job exemplified the ultimate irony: He was a man who couldn't solve his problems or control his vices, yet he had been placed in a position to help others find the will to do both.

Shortly after arriving in Omaha, Trout looked up his prison crony. They hit it off immediately, as if they'd known each other since childhood. Sometimes, they spoke on the phone. Other times, they met for a leisurely summer lunch at a courtyard park adjacent to the Hall of Justice. In fact, they had their first face-to-face visit as free men at the courtyard.

Trout paused for a sip of water.

It was at that meeting, Trout continued, that Steve bragged about his job at the Eppley Institute. Steve's eyes sparkled with excitement when he began sharing his secret: the existence of a "fantastic poison" that was impossible to detect in the body. A very small amount could kill many, many people. What's more, one molecule was enough to cause cancer to grow.

CANCER! Steve envisioned marketing the poison on the street, Trout told the hushed courtroom: "He talked about the potential of selling it to someone who might want to kill someone else."

Spellbound by the incredible story, everyone in the courtroom wanted Trout to go on except Corrigan. He'd had enough. He jumped up in protest, accusing the prosecutor of posing "leading and suggestive" questions. The judge overruled the objection.

According to Trout, Steve said he had a use for the poison himself; he needed to kill somebody.

"Did he say whom?" Cooper asked.

Corrigan popped out of his chair again. Objection, Your Honor. Objection.

Again, the judge overruled him.

"Yes," Trout answered. "He told me he wanted to kill his former girlfriend. He talked about sending a box of candy to the home of his former girlfriend and her family as a belated wedding gift. And the material [candy] he would send would have the substance in it."

Involuntarily, several jurors glanced at Steve. Their thoughts were written all over their faces. Candy? Despicable! He had to know the children would beg for some.

On the weekend before the poisoning, Trout and Steve met at the courtyard for another of their chats: murder over lunch. This time, Steve introduced a new scheme to extinguish the burning in his heart. Trout explained: "He told me that he planned to enter his former girl-friend's home and put the substance in food. He told me that he would enter the house either through a bedroom or kitchen window and go into the house when they weren't home and put the substance into material in the refrigerator." After discussing, at length, the "various ways" a person might ingest the poison, Steve settled on pouring the cancer-causing agent in milk, juice, or cottage cheese.

The ex-con claimed he didn't know Steve went through with the vindictive plot until October 13, the day the defendant called him from Texas, looking for ways to sneak out of the country.

At the end of Trout's testimony, Cooper inquired: "Did you report, at any time, any of these conversations to any law enforcement authorities?"

"I did not."

"Why not?"

"It was so bizarre, the whole idea. I felt that it was just so much hot air, just ridiculous. I didn't put any credibility in it. The *Omaha World-Herald* was sent to me from time to time after I had left, and in one of those issues it talked about these deaths."

"At that time," Cooper asked, "why did you not come forward with what you knew?"

"I didn't want to get involved in it. I'm on

parole. It could raise difficulties for me in my life."

On that selfish note, Defense Attorney Corrigan dove into his cross-examination, returning to the witness's criminal past to urge jurors to give Trout—the con artist, the thief, the former convict—no credibility. Regarding Trout's claim to having a master's degree when he applied at the Nebraska Department of Education, Corrigan asked:

"Was there some sort of an advantage to having a master's . . . getting more pay?"

"Yes."

"You lied to help yourself?" Corrigan asked, pacing the floor in front of the witness stand.

"I did."

"And then, I take it, there was a misdemeanor charge filed in the Lancaster County Court and you entered a plea of guilty to a misdemeanor? Is that right?"

"Right. No contest."

"And then you got another job working for the family planning division of Lancaster County?"

"No, no, sir."

"Who was that?"

"Family Service Association."

"Did you tell them about the problem that you had with your father or the problem that you had with the false degrees?"

"I told them about the problem with the Nebraska Department of Education. Yes."

Corrigan stopped pacing and stared at Trout: "How long was it before you started embezzling there?"

"Oh, perhaps a year."

"And then, eventually, you entered a plea of guilty to the charge of embezzlement and received penal time . . . is that correct?"

"Yes."

"And when you got down to the penitentiary, isn't it kind of unusual for a person to go directly from the orientation program to the trustees' dorm?"

"I don't know whether it is or not."

"Did you assist in testifying, or at least, so to speak, blowing the whistle against someone down at the penitentiary to get yourself into the T-dorm?"

"No, I did not."

"Danny Wade? Does that ring any bells with you?"

Trout thought for a second: "Yes, I remember Danny. Yes."

"Did Mr. Wade get in some problems down at the penitentiary as a result of statements that you gave the police department or the penal authorities?"

"Yes."

Obviously, Trout had cut a deal with prison officials and seemed to be in the habit of using people to stay out of trouble.

As he was about to step down from the stand, Trout looked, apologetically, at Steve: "I have always liked Steve a great deal. I think he has a good mind. I was, and am, interested in Steve's welfare."

With Trout, Cooper had solidly linked Steve to the murders and had established premeditation in the cruelest sense. Unless a juror or two doubted the embezzler's sincerity.

Once back in his cell, Steve's stone face came off. He angrily denounced his attorney for not being tougher on Trout and swore at the prosecutor for not charging Trout with murder, too. What a double-cross! Couldn't the prosecutor see the witness had participated in planning the poisoning? He coconspired! Trout said it himself. Trout sold him out.

Pastor Lueck's teaching duties prevented him from attending the trial, but he learned the essence of the day's testimony while visiting Steve in the evenings. That night, Steve recited his version of Trout's involvement. He claimed to his clergyman friend it was Trout who had encouraged him to steal the poison for both of them and it was Trout who had suggested he could use it to kill. Steve alleged Trout had forgotten, on the stand, that he repeatedly had telephoned the East Omahan's home in the days preceding the poisoning, wondering if he'd gone through with the plan.

"He was coaxing me," Steve claimed, arguing like a jailhouse attorney. "When he called me, he was asking me to do it."

Twenty-nine

FOLLOWING BILL TROUT'S APPEARANCE, Prosecutor Sam Cooper plunged into the medical aspects of the case with a parade of doctors: the family physicians, the neurologists, the pediatricians, the toxicologists, the pathologists, and the hematologist who had solved part of the mystery with blood transfusions. They testified about platelets and histology slides; decerebrate posturing and spinal taps; dextrose water and intracranial pressure monitors. Their presentations resembled a series of lectures for the man-on-the-street. Anytime the prosecutor noticed a juror's face twitch with confusion, he instructed the witness to back up and repeat the explanation.

To ensure that the jurors grasped how the medical gobbledegook translated into nightmarish consequences, Cooper introduced Dr. Ernest Summers. It had been over a year since the veterinarian had treated Levi and Cleops, but his eyes still watered. Asked about Levi the dog, he told the jury: "It died pretty horribly. Right before it died, it was very depressed. It could not lift its head; could not stand up; was vomiting a bloody, mucousy, frothy-type vomitus; was passing lots of blood by the rectum . . . a very foul, fetid odor coming from the bowels."

Cleops the cat?

It cried and threw its head back again and again when it lost its balance, the vet testified. Ultimately, it, too, lost all strength in its legs.

Cooper left it up to the jurors to imagine what the D.M.N. had done to Chad and Duane in their last hours alive.

Since the medical aspects of the deaths were not in contention, Corrigan asked few questions of the string of doctors.

To erase any doubt Steve had had access to D.M.N. at the Eppley Institute, the prosecutor ushered in Terrence A. Lawson, a Briton with a Ph.D. related to cancer research. Of the scientists employed at the research center, he worked the closest with Steve. In a heavy British accent, Lawson testified that employees stored the D.M.N. in a locked refrigerator, but the key was kept in a receptacle next to the refrigerator. Security was so lax, no one appeared to be in charge of knowing the amount of D.M.N. on hand.

It was Corrigan's turn to cross-examine. Instead of challenging the defendant's access to

D.M.N., he inquired if D.M.N. was present in cooked bacon.

"Yes," Lawson said, nodding.

Was it in Scotch whiskey?

"I'm afraid so. Yes." The courtroom erupted into laughter.

In the same vein, the defense attorney pulled out a *Los Angeles Times* service article that ran in the *Omaha World-Herald* just a few days before. The lead stated: "A renewal of interest in a cancer-causing agent found in trace amounts of beer has been sparked by the Food and Drug Administration's release of a list of twenty-eight beers said to contain the carcinogen, known as dimethylnitrosamine."

Corrigan shrugged his shoulders at the jurors: What else did the jury need to know? D.M.N. was in everything: bacon, whiskey, beer. Were beer drinkers dying from dimethylnitrosamine poisoning? Of course not. So how could Chad and Duane have died from D.M.N.? It was all folly.

Thirty

PROSECUTOR SAM COOPER believed he was well on his way toward convincing the jury that Steve Harper was the murderer, and as the second week of the trial neared an end, he confidently walked out into the hallway and returned with Dr. Ronald Shank. After asking the witness a series of brief questions to give everyone a general idea of his role in the case, the prosecutor put up a large chart on an easel. It read:

	G	. . .	GUANINE
DNA	A	. . .	ADENINE
BASES	T	. . .	THYMINE
	C	. . .	CYTOSINE
	5	. . .	METHYLCYTOSINE

"All right," Cooper began. "Would you tell us what the function of the DNA molecule is? Everybody has DNA molecules . . . is that correct?"

"Yes."

Cooper gestured with a hand for Shank to continue.

"All genetic information for every living cell is stored in the molecule DNA. The genetic information is stored in a chemical code based on the adjacent positions of those five bases that you see there: guanine, adenine, thymine, cytosine, and 5 methylcytosine."

Shank pointed to the chart.

"The genetic characteristics of every cell are defined by the sequence in which those bases occur in DNA. These bases are held together against the backbone, which is composed of two kinds of chemical groups: One is a sugar and the other a phosphate. So the backbone is a sugar-phosphate chain. DNA is very repetitive; the chemical groups repeat themselves. A sugar molecule group is connected to a phosphate group, then a sugar again and then a phosphate. This DNA chain allows the bases to be put together in a given fashion. Each sugar contains one of the bases: guanine, adenine, thymine, cytosine or 5 methylcytosine. What we were looking for was the presence of abnormal bases, bases in positions where they shouldn't be. That would be indicative of exposure to a very strong methylating agent compound."

Normally, witnesses responded to specific questions with short answers. They were discouraged from lengthy narratives. But Corrigan wasn't objecting. His scheme to ambush Shank and Renate Kimbrough was set.

Shank explained that a methylating compound partly consisted of a carbon with three hydrogens: CH_3. When introduced into the body, the three hydrogens, CH_3, attached themselves to DNA to form methylated DNA. Dimethylnitrosamine was a methylating compound because its formula was:

$$CH_3 \atop \diagdown \atop N - N = O \atop \diagup \atop CH_3$$

Since there were two CH_3's in dimethylnitrosamine, Shank went on, it was called "di," for two "methyl." The N–N=O stood for the substance nitrosamine.

Cooper sensed he should interject. It wasn't necessary for jurors to understand every scientific twist, merely certain key links.

"So, what you're looking for is one of the G's, A's, T's—one of the five bases—that has CH_3 attached to it?"

"Yes," Shank said. "We would be looking for methylguanine rather than just guanine."

"In order to run those tests," Cooper guided him, "is it first necessary to isolate the DNA molecule?"

"Yes, it is."

"Who did that in this case?"

"Mrs. Deborah Herron."

Cooper excused Shank temporarily to let Herron testify. While someone summoned the researcher's senior graduate student, Cooper took down the chart on DNA bases and replaced it with one listing the blind test samples.

Once in the witness box, Herron explained that she and Shank were able to isolate DNA from only five of the eight tissue samples because the rest were too small to analyze or too damaged by whatever had attacked the victims. All five usable samples were tested for methylated DNA.

"How many times, approximately, have you run through this process to isolate and purify DNA in tissue?" Cooper inquired.

"I've done at least a thousand isolations of different tissue samples."

"And where did you learn that process?"

"In Dr. Shank's laboratory."

"With reference to toxicology No. 23675, kidney tissue. Did you find methylated DNA?"

"No, we did not."

"With reference to 23677, liver tissue, did you find methylated DNA there?"

"Yes."

"With reference to 23851, liver tissue, did you find methylated DNA?"

"No."

"23853, kidney?"

"No."

"23854, liver?"

"No."

"26689, liver?"

"No."

"26690, liver?"

"No."

"26691, kidney?"

"No."

At the end of the exchange, Herron, at the instruction of the prosecutor, walked to the chart and drew a purple circle around the specimen number contaminated with a methylating compound. Then she wrote "methylated DNA" next to the circled number.

Cooper already knew the researchers had succeeded in detecting methylated DNA in Duane Johnson's liver, No. 23677 in the blind test, but he planned to let Dr. Renate Kimbrough reveal the results as part of her testimony.

Corrigan consulted his assistant, chemist John McGuire, before cross-examining Herron. He aimed at the most vulnerable spot in her testimony.

"Just a couple of questions. Do you isolate DNA and search for methylated DNA routinely on livers and hearts and kidneys of *HUMANS?*"

"Not humans, no."

"How many times have you run these kind of tests on *HUMAN* organs?"

"This was the first time I've done it on human tissue."

"So," Corrigan asked dubiously, "the thousands of other times you have dealt with experimental rats?"

"Yes, and other rodents mainly."

"Well, as far as you know, this is the first time this particular test has ever been attempted with kidneys, hearts, and livers of *HUMAN* beings?"

"Yes, this particular analysis."

Corrigan sat down. No further questions.

As far as the defense attorney could tell, everyone was still presuming the methylating substance *HAD* to be D.M.N., dimethylnitrosamine. According to his expert, there were many methylating substances that caused methylated D.N.A. When Shank returned to the stand, Corrigan used his cross-examination to prepare the groundwork for his key witness, Dr. Werner Spitz.

"In your testing," Corrigan asked, "did you actually find, BEYOND ANY DOUBT, dimethylnitrosamine?"

Shank hadn't expected the question: "We did not look for dimethylnitrosamine itself. We found evidence that the tissue had been exposed to a methylating agent."

"And I take it that dimethylnitrosamine is a methylating agent?"

"Yes, it's metabolized to a methylating agent."

"There are many other substances that do the same thing . . . are there not?"

"Yes."

"Some known and some unknown? Would that be fair to say?"

"I think so, yes."

"Could you give us any idea of how many other substances, besides dimethylnitrosamine, will give you this result in the DNA examination?"

"Twenty or more compounds."

Corrigan bowed his head pensively to give the jurors a chance to digest the researcher's last statement: TWENTY OR MORE COMPOUNDS. Not one, but TWENTY OR MORE.

"Would it be fair to say," Corrigan continued, "that the results of your analysis are really that twenty or more substances could have been the methylating agent?"

"Yes."

Corrigan's perceptive questioning left in doubt the value of Shank's elaborate tests and the prosecutor's only physical evidence.

Prosecutor Cooper asked one last question before Shank was dismissed: Did the witness know which methylating agents more likely caused the DNA change in the tissue?

Shank nodded and disclosed that he had sent a list of the eight "water-soluble methylating toxicants" to Renate Kimbrough at CDC.

She was to testify the following week.

Thirty-one

EVEN AS THE TRIAL of Steve Harper commenced in Omaha, Renate Kimbrough worked feverishly on the Midwest poisoning in her Atlanta laboratory. Her job at the trial was to close the loop: testify, convincingly, that dimethylnitrosamine *HAD* to be the poison. To accomplish that, she studied the characteristics of scores of compounds: carbon tetrachloride, tetrachloroethane, methotrexate, paradimethylaminobenzaldehyde, pyrrolizidine, arsenic, selenium, paraquat, phosphorus, acetaminophen, and hydrazine. The doctor-researcher also scrutinized Shank's list of water-soluble methylating toxicants: methyl methane sulfonate, dimethylsulfate, dimethylnitrosamine, N-methyl-N'-nitro-N-nitrosoguanidine, 1,2-dimethyl hydrazine, methyl chloride, methyl bromide, and methyl iodide. Her final analysis went into a report she titled "Summary of Evaluation Which Led to the Conclusion that Dimethylnitrosamine

Caused the Outbreak of Illness in the Johnson and Shelton Families in Omaha, Nebraska." Upon flying into Omaha on Sunday, September 30, she handed Cooper her report.

At ten the next morning, Kimbrough took the stand, ready to defend her thesis and deflect whatever the defense attorney had up his sleeve. She sat erect with confidence and made direct eye contact with anyone who addressed her. She knew the defense would try to rattle her, but she wasn't worried. Hadn't she grown up dodging bombs during World War II?

Next to Trout, Corrigan considered Kimbrough the most damaging witness. She was the only individual willing to stake her reputation on the assertion that dimethylnitrosamine had killed Chad and Duane. From the outset, the defense attorney informed the judge he considered her unqualified to testify as an expert and he planned to object to her entire testimony.

For over an hour, Cooper had Kimbrough detail her initial involvement in the case and the tests she conducted on rats given substances from the home of Sandy and Duane Johnson.

Next, the prosecutor directly confronted Corrigan's campaign of suggesting that the deaths might be an accident.

"Based on your training and your experience and your research of the literature," Cooper said, "do you have an opinion as to whether or not argon, hydrogen, oxygen, nitrogen, carbon dioxide, or any of those inert gases in combination could cause the symptoms and pathology that you observed in these cases?"

"Could not have."

"Just a second," Corrigan cut in. "I think that question calls for a yes or no answer."

"Doctor," the judge asked, "do you have an opinion in that regard?"

"Yes, I do have an opinion."

"Would you ask what the opinion is?" the judge instructed Cooper.

"What is your opinion?"

"I object, Your Honor," Corrigan said.

"The objection is overruled."

"Now," Cooper stated, "you can answer the question."

"From the review of the slides and all the information, I have to conclude that none of these gases could have caused the illness in the patients."

"What about anhydrous ammonia?"

"That could not have caused this either."

"May I have the same continuing objection to all this testimony, Your Honor?" Corrigan asked.

"You may."

Cooper resumed his questioning: "Were you able to develop any information which would indicate to you that this was an airborne disease of some type?"

"The same objection, Your Honor," Corrigan said.

"The same ruling."

"The illness was selective in that only certain people became ill," she explained, "but others who were in the same building and in the same surroundings did not. Anytime you have an airborne illness, it should affect anybody that takes in the same air."

"Were you able to determine whether or not the outbreak in this case could have been caused by Legionnaires' disease or a similar bacteria?"

Corrigan, again, objected. Again, his objection was overruled.

"The pathology findings in Legionnaires' disease are different," Kimbrough pointed out.

"All right, Doctor, based on the information you received from the Douglas County Health Department; John Wiley; Dr. Jacobson; the pathologists involved; the attending physicians you talked to; the medical charts of all the patients; the epidemiological investigation; the histology slides that you viewed of Duane Johnson and Chad Shelton; the photographs of the organs as provided to you by the pathologists; your consultations with other physicians, toxicologists, and chemists; your consultations with Dr. MaGee; your medical research and your experience and training, have you reached an opinion within reasonable medical certainty as to what the substance was that caused the deaths and illnesses in this case?"

"Yes, I have."

"And what is that conclusion?"

Corrigan was already out of his seat: "Your Honor. I make the same objection."

"The objection is overruled. You may answer."

"I concluded that the illness and deaths were caused by dimethylnitrosamine."

At Cooper's request, Kimbrough explained how she compared the various compounds to reach her conclusion. For instance, she said, poisoning by methyl chloride, methyl bromide, and methyl iodide usually occurs following inhalation and predominantly affects the central nervous system. Methyl methane sulfonate, dimethylsulfate, and N-methyl-N'-nitro-N-nitrosoguanidine do not cause the type of liver damage observed in the victims. N-methyl-N'-nitro-N-nitrosoguanidine is acutely less toxic than dimethylnitrosamine. Dimethylsulfate is known to break down to sulfuric acid and methanol in water, and the victims would have noticed it in the beverages they consumed. Dimethylnitrosamine is the only chemical that could have been in the lemonade.

Since the wall clock indicated there were only a few minutes left before the noon hour, Cooper indulged in a little courtroom tit for tat. He asked Kimbrough if dimethylnitrosamine in beer, as the defense implied the week before, posed a toxic threat. A smirk appeared on Kimbrough's face. She testified that Duane Johnson would have had to drink fifty thousand gallons of beer in a short time to produce the toxic level that killed him. Courtroom spectators burst out laughing.

After lunch, it was Corrigan's turn at the star witness.

With a combination of biting questions and short commentaries, the public defender portrayed Kimbrough as a researcher trying to be someone she was not qualified to be: a pathologist. Under the law, he expounded, pathologists are charged with determining cause and manner of death. The witness was trying to pass herself off as a pathologist because she had conducted "a few autopsies." She was neither a pathologist, the attorney pointed out caustically, nor a forensic medical examiner, who specializes in the criminal investigation of death. Was she a fraud? A charlatan? Corrigan didn't ask the question directly, but hoped the words crystallized in the jurors' minds. When it was time for him to present his case, it would be obvious Dr. Werner Spitz was a medical examiner. One of the best.

With every question, Corrigan jabbed at Kimbrough's credentials:

"Do you know how long it takes to become certified as a forensic pathologist?"

"No, I don't."

"You've told us that you've reached an opinion as to the cause of death in this particular case and that it's dimethylnitrosamine. Now,

you're familiar with the contents of the autopsy
reports that have been written by Dr. Greene
and Dr. Schenken with regard to two of the people involved in this case, are you not?"

"Yes, I am."

"All right. Now both of those people testified
that in their opinion the cause of death was necrosis of the liver, but they went no further.
Now you have gone further, is that correct?"

"I have really not gone any further. They
both said that it was caused by a toxin, a poison
. . . that this type of necrosis of the liver could
not have been caused by an infection."

"I understand that, but—"

Kimbrough interrupted: ". . . but the only
thing that I would go further is to try and identify the specific chemical that I think caused
this particular liver lesion."

Corrigan changed the subject and turned to
questioning the health of the CDC rats used in
the early stages of the investigation.

"Now, these rats that you used to put the
substances in . . . did they have anything genetically wrong with them?"

"The rats we've had for many years. We
have our own breeding colonies at the Centers
for Disease Control."

"Do they have anything wrong with them,
genetically?"

"They do have some abnormalities which
occur occasionally, but so do most of the other
strains that are commercially available. I've

worked with these rats since 1962 and I'm quite familiar with their background disease level. I'm able to separate that from any effects that are caused by poisons. As they get old, they get spontaneous tumors, particularly mammary-gland tumors."

Corrigan shifted his line of questioning again, this time to accuse the witness of taking too many things for granted in concluding the deaths resulted from foul play. Raising his voice, he charged that she assumed the lemon-ade pitcher had been washed, she assumed that no one else became ill, and she assumed the poison was water soluble, hence excluding non-water-soluble methylating substances from her analysis.

"Now," he said, lowering his voice, "did you also assume, in reaching your opinion, that a thorough analysis was done by the health people of the plumbing of the Johnson home?"

"I did not assume that," Kimbrough shot back, "because I don't think that the deaths and illnesses had anything to do with the plumb-ing."

Some of the jurors were beginning to peek at their watches. It was almost 4 P.M. Corrigan told Judge Murphy he had only a question or two more.

"There are each year a number of unex-plained deaths around the country, for various reasons, are there not?"

"Yes, unfortunately, there are," Kimbrough responded.

"All right. I guess what I'm trying to get to, Doctor, is that there are a lot of things the experts don't know are out there, about diseases and about foreign substances and their effect on the human body?"

The witness could see through his question and didn't bite.

"There are certain things that we do know," she said, smiling. "Sometimes, it's the way the investigations are conducted that give negative results."

Her answer angered Corrigan.

"Have you ever been wrong, Doctor?"

"Yes."

"We all have, haven't we?"

"Yes."

"You're dealing in an area that has really just developed over the last twenty years. Am I correct?"

"There is more interest now in toxicology and more people have gotten involved," Kimbrough explained, "but toxicology has been around ever since Socrates was poisoned."

The philosopher had killed himself with hemlock in 399 B.C.

For all practical purposes, Kimbrough capped the state's case. In all, Cooper called over thirty witnesses to the stand, some for the important but brief purpose of identifying a photograph or document. And he entered into evidence over eighty exhibits: vials, slides, diagrams, medical records, autopsy reports, DNA charts.

Some evidence was never introduced, such as the demonology pictures that Steve had sent to Sandy. The series of cutouts would have only helped the defendant set the stage for an insanity defense.

Thirty-two

DEFENSE ATTORNEY LAWRENCE CORRIGAN was depending on Wayne County Chief Medical Examiner Dr. Werner U. Spitz to discredit, if not decimate and embarrass, Renate Kimbrough. The world-renowned expert on death staunchly believed he could never say dimethylnitrosamine had killed Chad and Duane. He'd never wavered from that view, even in the days just before the trial when Corrigan flew to Detroit to rehearse his testimony.

Already, the doctor had been tremendously helpful. Corrigan consulted Spitz several times during the testimony of the prosecution's key witnesses. Just knowing what to ask meant the world in such a complicated case. After Kimbrough testified, the public defender spoke briefly with Spitz, then sent him Kimbrough's report by overnight carrier.

The medical examiner was due to arrive in Omaha this morning to lead off the defense at 1 P.M. But everything fell apart that day.

About 8 A.M., the phone rang in Corrigan's office as he made last-minute preparations. It was his wife, bearing bad news: Spitz was not coming.

WHAT! How could that be? Corrigan felt as if he'd been hit in the head with a brick. Stunned, he instructed his wife to repeat the medical examiner's every word. She spoke slowly: "He said he was in Chicago and that he was not coming."

Why would he back out? Why did he travel halfway and turn back?

A short time later, the phone rang again in Corrigan's office. This time, it was Spitz himself. The doctor calmly stated he was at the Chicago airport and the plane bound for Omaha had left. He was about to board a plane to return home to Detroit.

By then, the public defender's shock had turned to anger.

"Why aren't you coming?"

"It would be a very bad mistake for you to call me as a witness," Spitz said with a German accent much thicker than that of his compatriot from CDC. "My testimony would hurt you."

"Doctor, the only thing I am going to put you on the stand for is to have you repeat what you've already told me: that there could be approximately thirty other substances that cause methylated DNA and dimethylnitrosamine is one of them. That is all I want you to say."

"Well," the doctor repeated, "I am not going to help you very much. I know you don't want me. You will thank me someday for not showing up."

"I will not thank you," Corrigan interrupted. "Now, please continue your trip to Omaha. I want to personally discuss your testimony with you."

"No," Spitz said, and hung up.

Long after the trial ended, Spitz vaguely explained: "Something that morning made me turn back. I was getting pangs of conscience. I couldn't cope with the idea of saying something that was untrue. If somebody is left high and dry, too bad. You do what is morally correct."

Without Spitz, Steve's case seemed doomed.

That afternoon in the courtroom, Corrigan sheepishly whispered in his client's ear. Steve wasn't too surprised at the bad news: nothing seemed to be going his way.

Corrigan's first witness—Richard Rensch, an assistant public defender in Corrigan's office —caused the defendant further consternation.

Standing in front of the jury box, Rensch displayed a plastic container and several drinking glasses similar to those used at the Johnson home on the day of the poisoning. According to one witness, the sixty-four-ounce pitcher appeared a fourth full when the victims began drinking from it, meaning it contained about seventeen ounces. Rensch demonstrated that seventeen ounces of liquid filled one average-sized glass and part of a second one. Duane Johnson alone was believed to have consumed more than one glass.

Obviously, argued Corrigan, there wasn't enough lemonade to go around to all the victims. A second batch of lemonade must have been made, probably at a time the family was home and Steve could not enter the house without detection. Either that, or investigators were wrong in surmising the poison was in the lemonade.

Steve thought the demonstration dumb, a waste of time.

Cooper wrinkled his face like a boy holding up a dead skunk and stared at Rensch: "You went to law school three years for that?"

Corrigan's next maneuver was even more incredible than the pitcher-and-glass act.

Suddenly, he announced a surprise witness. He called her an "alibi witness" and escorted her into the courtroom to get his client off the hook. Steve apparently had thought his defense needed a boost, for it was he who had concocted her existence two days before.

After swearing to tell the truth and nothing but the truth, Omahan Susan Gaston claimed she and her husband were with Steve at a lounge on the evening of the poisonings. Gaston testified she and her husband had arrived at the bar about 5:30 P.M. on September 9, 1978, and were joined by their longtime friend about 7 P.M. The three stayed until 2 A.M. The timing was critical since the state contended Steve had broken into the Johnson home between 8:30 P.M. September 9 and 2 A.M. September 10.

The woman's brief testimony concluded Corrigan's anemic presentation. In all, Steve's defense totaled thirty-seven minutes.

By 2 P.M. Judge Murphy ordered both sides to present their closing arguments.

Since the start of the trial, Cooper had kept a small trial notebook at his side to jot down thoughts to include in his closing statement. He reviewed those notes before approaching the jurors.

"Mrs. Gaston should be given no credibility," Cooper began, throwing his arms up in the air. "She miraculously appears like she was beamed down from above. If she was so concerned for her friend Mr. Harper, why did she wait so long and let her friend sit in jail for a year?

"I'm not trying to appeal to your emotions. I think we could have done that a lot of times during the course of the trial. I want to appeal to your common sense."

The prosecutor put both hands on the jury box railing to force the jurors to focus on what he was about to say next:

"Somebody asked: 'Well, why didn't anybody test for dimethylnitrosamine?' Dimethylnitrosamine metabolizes rapidly in the body, so you don't have dimethylnitrosamine. You're not going to find that substance as a substance.

"Dr. Kimbrough got on the stand the other day and said: 'This is my background. This is what I've done.' She's considered, by the World Health Organization, to have some competence because she works with them on cancer research. She told you what kind of work she was involved in. This isn't somebody that we just hauled out of a lab someplace that had no experience. And Mr. Corrigan must have spent twenty-five minutes with her, making sure that you all realized that she was not a forensic pathologist. She never said she was. She said: 'I worked for a forensic pathologist in Germany. I've got some background in that. I'm a physician, but here's what I do. I work in trying to do exactly what was done here: Get information from other sources, find out what's the best way to determine what happened, and then contact other experts.'"

Cooper moved to the center of the floor, in front of the judge's bench:

"I'll submit to you that we've proved beyond any doubt whatsoever that what was used was dimethylnitrosamine. This case is unusual, perhaps unlike any ever before in criminal history. This is the first case of murder by cancer, ever."

Cooper paused to let that wicked thought sink in. Then he continued.

"Based on the evidence you've heard, there's only one possible verdict you're going to come in with. You'll find that Mr. Harper did exactly what he's charged with."

Inadvertently, the prosecutor characterized the case as "murder by cancer." Steve's plan was to inoculate people with a cancer-causing compound. Chad and Duane died of the substance's toxicity.

In his closing argument, Defense Attorney Corrigan asked the jurors to pardon him for introducing a witness so unexpectedly at the eleventh hour and urged them to give Mrs. Gaston's testimony as much weight as any other witness. He reminded them, however, that the burden of proving the charges rested entirely with the prosecution.

At that point, Corrigan reverted to his doubt campaign. He charged that the investigation into the deaths was incomplete and a number of possible causes were never explored.

"To top the thing off," the public defender exclaimed, "they bring in Mr. William Trout. I'm going to have to say something about Mr. Trout. I can't believe him. He's a liar. I'll say one thing: He appeared to be very intelligent on this stand. There isn't any way of shaking Mr. Trout. I never really tried. Mr. Trout says he, not one hundred yards from here, sat down and listened to this man say that he was going to kill these people with something stolen from the Eppley Research Center and doesn't do a thing."

Placing his hands on his hips, the public defender paced the floor for a moment without saying a word. Then he whirled to face the jurors:

"We've had experts and experts and experts. Mr. Cooper said they were going to bring in the greatest experts in the world, and, by God, they did. I have to say that when you're talking about the caliber of Dr. Greene, Dr. Shubik, Dr. Shank, fantastic people. Dr. Schenken, the pathologist. His job is to determine what causes death. He's an expert, he's done thousands of autopsies. Dr. Greene's got the same job. They've done their training, and they've been here. Did they testify that dimethylnitrosamine was the cause? They're experts. They had all of the things available to them that could be made available, including Mrs. Kimbrough's report, or Dr. Kimbrough's report. But they didn't testify to it, they won't testify to it, because it's . . . it's . . . it's sheer folly."

Corrigan paused for a moment.

"Now, if Dr. Schenken was asked a question, if Dr. Greene was asked a question, if Dr. Shank was asked a question, the answer was definite, deliberate. If it required a yes or no, we got a yes or no. If Dr. Kimbrough was asked a question, God forbid, because you've got to hang on to your pants. You're going to be ten minutes waiting for her not to answer the question. And I submit, ladies and gentlemen, if there's another witness that you, perhaps, should be ignoring, it's Dr. Kimbrough.

"Now, this case bothers me as a father and it bothers me as a human being. The only thing that could be worse is if you could take a look at this evidence and let a goofy theory, and that's what it is, stand and just make worse a horrible situation that's very sad. I hope to God that you won't."

Before returning to his seat, Corrigan remarked, with a slight tone suggesting unfairness, that judicial rules allowed the state to make a few additional comments.

Rising, Cooper pointed a finger at Corrigan: "If the defense has so many other things that might have caused the illnesses and deaths, why didn't Mr. Corrigan call his own experts? Why didn't he conduct his own tests?"

"Objection, Your Honor," Corrigan yelled. "Mr. Cooper is out of line." The judge overruled the public defender.

Walking by the pitcher and glasses used earlier by the defense, the prosecutor shook his head bewilderedly: "I don't know what kind of mind does this. What the man does is go into a home in the middle of the night, opens up an icebox, sees a pitcher like that, and pours what he knows to be a carcinogenic drug into it."

Cooper carefully picked up a child's training cup and held it up: "And sitting right next to it is something that looks like this. He knows that there are kids in that house. That takes a terribly, terribly compelling motive to do something like that. And there's only one person on the face of the earth that you've heard about that has that kind of a motive."

The prosecutor had just sat down when Judge Murphy turned to the jurors and entrusted them with Steve's fate. By the same time the following day, they had reached a verdict.

Steve stood impassively, staring straight ahead, as the jury foreman announced guilty verdicts on all five counts.

Bill Trout made the difference. Before his testimony, the jurors divulged later, everyone had agreed with Corrigan: The crime was too outlandish to believe. Only in the movies did people sneak into homes through bedroom windows. And only in the smutty supermarket tabloids existed undetectable chemicals to get rid of former lovers. Trout changed their thinking.

Prosecutor Cooper was not a man to derive pleasure out of convicting individuals who faced death. Still, it felt good to win, to put all the scientific pieces together. In Cooper's opinion, the verdict easily could have gone the other way: In the judicial system, guilt didn't guarantee convictions.

Cooper was surprised his counterpart had not tried to confuse the jurors with a love triangle theory. To Cooper, the possibility wasn't out of the question. Sandy's own family believed she may have rekindled her relationship with Steve. And there was her initial statement to Detective Miller: Steve was a quiet individual not prone to violence. True, there existed no proof of her involvement—Steve told Detective Greg Thompson that he had acted alone and Trout had mentioned no conspiracy—but nobody had spent enough time looking for coconspirators. Everyone had been too busy trying to identify the poison and understand the mechanics of the toxin. How preoccupied, oblivious, had they all been? No one knew, but it troubled Cooper enough to request that prison authorities keep an eye on Steve's mail to ascertain if he and Sandy corresponded in the weeks following the trial.

Thirty-three

A MONTH AFTER THE TRIAL, Steve Harper entered Judge James Murphy's courtroom neatly dressed in gray slacks and a brown sweater vest pulled over a white shirt. A deputy walked next to him on each side and one trailed behind him. Just in case.

In the gallery sat Jesse and Eva Lou Harper, stoically. At the rear of the courtroom, against the wall, anxiously stood Detective K. G. Miller and Detective Greg Thompson. None of the victims or their relatives emerged from their agony.

For over thirty minutes, Judge Murphy recited the pros and cons of sentencing Steve to death. His inflection gave no clue of his decision. Finally, in a firm but halting voice, he pronounced the poisoning "coldly calculated" and "pitiless" and observed that Chad Shelton and his uncle had suffered "slow, agonizing deaths."

Steve should die on the electric chair at 6 A.M. on February 15, 1980.

For a moment, no one spoke. Everyone appeared to be holding their breath. Tears rolled out of Eva Lou's eyes. Her firstborn would die.

The judge spoke directly to Steve: "I know from your emotional letters to me that you are not at peace with yourself. I hope you find peace in your next life."

Detective Miller couldn't suppress a slight smile. He looked forward to seeing Steve dragged, kicking and screaming, to the electric chair. He deserved every kilowatt.

Book Five

A
WAY
OUT

Thirty-four

DEATH HAD SEEMED IMMINENT in the courtroom. It always did. But when Steven Harper arrived at the Nebraska State Penitentiary in Lincoln, Nebraska, few people there believed he would keep his appointment with "Old Sparky" in the basement of the administration building. And they were right; February 1980 came and went without Steve being strapped into the crude, homemade wooden electric chair as ordered by Judge James Murphy. Not since June 25, 1959, at 12:05 A.M.—when nineteen-year-old Charles Starkweather had absorbed the chair's three thousand volts for a series of murders attributed to him and his girlfriend—had a convicted murderer been executed. Instead of joining the exclusive club of twenty who had been hanged or electrocuted in the state since 1903, Steve fell in step with a legion of modern convicts whose appeals devoured years. Almost before Steve's mug shot went up in the guardhouse where the "screws" controlled the door locks to death row, his appeal switched to automatic pilot.

In the meantime, death row became home to "Inmate 32533," or "The Kool-Aid Kid," as the guards called Steve among themselves. He was one of a dozen murderers whose life revolved around concrete-block cells the size of a walk-in closet. Each cubicle was equipped with a miniature combination stainless steel toilet, sink, and mirror; a black army cot; a small desk with a bookshelf above it; a black metal footlocker for socks and odds and ends; and a red fluorescent night-light.

Many death row inmates preferred their cells barren, like their lives. Steve hung up a "Back to the Bible Scriptures" calendar and brought in a radio. At his bedside, he kept three Bibles, a book of hymns, and a Webster's Dictionary.

Most hours, Steve and his few amenities were sealed in with a green steel door. A small, rectangular bullet-resistant window on the door allowed the guards to peek in. When not locked in, Steve and the other death row prisoners were not permitted to mingle with the lifers or the general population of seven hundred thirty sad-eyed misfits packed into several brick structures built for four hundred eighty-eight.

On death row, in particular, every day seemed like the day before: the same guards, the same fake smiles, the same khaki clothes, the same clanging doors, the same routine—

eight steps to the shower, ten steps to the indoor activity room, twenty-nine steps to the eating hall one floor below. From the beginning, the isolation and monotony depressed Steve and thrust him into bouts of despair. Week after week, month after month, year after year, he sat on his cot in a stupor or walked in circles in his cell waiting for a doctor who didn't exist to perform surgery on his scars. He rarely used the outdoor yard, where inmates lifted weights, played basketball, and walked around the perimeter for exercise. He shied away from the showers, fearing he might be sexually assaulted. He even refused to eat regularly because he suspected the cooks of being homosexuals out to contaminate the mashed potatoes with the AIDS virus.

Most days, Steve resembled a starving Skid Row bum: His color was ashen, his face unshaven, and his clothes wrinkled.

During the brief periods that Steve thought of communicating with the outside world, he wrote obsessively to Vincent M. Powers, a Lincoln attorney assigned to keep him out of the electric chair. In one letter Steve wrote, "I am looking for my grandfather. He is in North Africa fighting the Nazi Germans." In closing, he revealed: "I am a priest now. My name is Father Stephanas. I give you absolution." In a later letter, he announced that he'd been made "Pope Stephanas I."

Once in a great while, Steve seemed cognizant of his hopeless fate. In one of those moments, he penned a short note to Detective K. G. Miller, pleading for help in getting his death sentence commuted. The investigator never wrote back, but he told his wife, "The audacity of that guy. I hope he burns in hell. That dirty rotten bastard."

For a long time the prison staff believed Steve was faking insanity. But, eventually, they became concerned enough to put him on powerful antipsychotic medication. Once his mind was fastened together with drugs, he ate with the other prisoners and obediently picked up his multiple daily doses of medication. But he still preferred spending most of his time in his cell.

Time did little for Steve. As he began his second decade on death row, the voices in his head got louder, bolder. In April 1990, he pulled out his tape recorder. For over an hour, he dictated in a hushed, raspy voice:

Dear Vince:

I want to tell you in this tape about two psychiatrists that came and talked to me a while ago. It's confusing to me and it frightens me. I cannot understand most of their questions. It was a man and a woman. They asked me where I was now. It's common knowledge. We are at Lincoln General Hospital and I've been here for a few years. I've been waiting to see Dr. Andersen, a surgeon, who is going to do plastic surgery on my scars. Then I will be released and I'll go back to Omaha.

I'm not sure because I have to wait and be told by one of the spirits. They tell me what to do all the time. Their commands used to be more awful and more intense. I was given medication. First they used to give me Stelazine. That stopped working so much they gave me Haldol. That stopped working so much and now I'm given Navane.

Sometimes the spirits tell me their name so I can recognize their voices. There is a spirit named Abedon. There is one called Apolian. There's Belile. Belsebub. There's Prince of the Power in the Air. One God of this World. One of them is Potentate. There's Constellation. Deity. Morning Star. Corner Stone. Jehovah Jira. Moses. Messenger Angel.

The spirits harass me. They pump gas threw the vents in my room. They have bad smell, bad odors. I smell them all the time. Sometimes there's an alcohol smell. Sometimes there's an ether smell. Or the smell of burned flesh.

That's all the information I have at this time. Hopefully, this gets to you.

Steve turned the tape off, then on again.

I'm a new creature, new creation. I've been reborn. Jehovah Jira told me all things are passed away.

In my head I hear a humming sound. Voices, spirits. I hear a lot of cussing towards me. Spirits accuse me of being a stupid son of a bitch. A dumb, ignorant motherfucker. A no-good Indian bitch. They call me skunk, squirrel. A dog.

Once in a great while, the spirits care. They need to show their face in the window of the door. Usually at night. Their eyes are usually red, white veins. I can usually see their blood vessels on the face. Their faces don't usually look like they have a color. Sometimes, they change appearance at the door. Sometimes, they'll be walking down the hallway and all of a sudden they come out of the wall. You've got to get out of the way. Sometimes, they'll just be a flash of color. Then, they'll disappear. I don't know why these things happen.

Thirty-five

STEVE AWOKE WITH a clear sense of himself and everything around him. He washed, shaved, combed his hair, and dressed in clean, pressed clothes. While momentarily out of his cell in the morning, an inmate noticed "he had a little more lift in his step than most days." Another thought he saw the death row hermit smile.

About two in the afternoon, Steve joined the other killers in the exercise yard outside. He hadn't done that in years. One of the prisoners urged him to put on a coat. It was December, not July.

"It's a nice day," Steve responded, his breath forming steam out of the cold winter air. "Oh yeah, it's a beautiful day!"

After socializing in the yard for half an hour, Steve returned to his cell.

At 4 P.M., he made his way downstairs to the mess hall for supper. Before leaving the eating area a short time later, he reached into a metal box protruding from the fortified guardhouse and retrieved his antipsychotic medication.

At 8 P.M., Steve walked out of his cell again. He hurried downstairs to the guardhouse, accepted his last dose of medication for the day and put it in his mouth, being very careful not to swallow.

Once back in D-9, he penned a quick letter to his parents on stationery with the preprinted message: "Wishing You a Beautiful Holiday Season." After inserting the note in a red envelope, he turned off the light and undressed down to his T-shirt, boxer shorts, and socks.

As soft music played on the radio, he located a stash of medication he'd been hoarding and ingested it. In bed, he pulled the covers over him and folded his arms on his stomach.

Sometime that night, the battered, tattered, malignant young life of Steven Roy Harper came to a slow end. Sandy's ghost could haunt him no more.

Epilogue
1993

THE NIGHTMARE WILL NEVER be over for Sallie and Bruce Shelton and Sherrie Johnson, since Steve's original plan—to commit murder by cancer—may still be fulfilled someday. They were once told, bluntly, that they stood a chance of contracting the disease, since their bodies took a tremendous blow from a substance known to modify DNA. Such modification is believed to lead slowly to tumor formation. The Sheltons are convinced someday they will die of cancer.

The uncertainty of the future devastated the Sheltons. Bruce yearned for another child but Sallie fought getting pregnant. She told the family: "I'm not going to live long enough to see it raised. I don't want anybody else raising my child." Their disagreement turned to acrimony, leading them to dissolve their marriage in 1988. Sallie remarried in 1991, but vows to remain childless.

Before the Sheltons divorced, they and Sandy Johnson filed a $40.5 million lawsuit against Eppley. The court threw it out, claiming there was no way the institute could have known Steve had intended to kill.

The entire ordeal embittered Sallie, who felt robbed of health, children, and savings. Sallie told the family: "I think Steve cheated us out of everything."

The poisonings barely fazed strong-willed Sandy. Her spirited relationship with men resumed with Bruce Marchant, the man she married after Duane died.

Despite volatile disagreements, Sandy and Bruce had a baby in 1980. Not long thereafter, the family moved into a spacious trailer house, which Bruce filled with new furniture, including a $1,000 couch.

As often happened in Sandy's life, things went terribly wrong one day in January 1982. Following an altercation, Bruce threw blankets over a kerosene heater to start a fire. Sandy and the children barely made it out alive.

Sandy filed for divorce. It was granted while her husband fought first-degree arson charges. Bruce was convicted, but served only a few days in jail.

Strangely, Sandy forgave him and they remarried. As expected, the union dissolved and the thirty-year-old mother of three filed for divorce, again, in 1983. It, too, was granted, ending Sandy's fourth nuptial tie.

Eventually, she married a fifth time and

moved to the East Coast. She keeps in touch with relatives in the Midwest.

Her mother, Jean, died in 1993. Dave Beard still lives in Omaha. Sandy's oldest brother survived the 1975 shooting, but one of the shotgun pellets wanders perilously behind an eye. Fourteen other pellets embedded in him tingle in the winter.

As for those who investigated or helped adjudicate the mysterious poisoning:

- Detective K. G. Miller retired from the Omaha Police Department in 1984. He died of cancer in 1989.
- Homicide Lieutenant Foster Burchard also retired from OPD. He now works in the property room of the Douglas County Sheriff's Office.
- Sam Cooper remains a "trial dog" with the Douglas County Prosecutor's Office. Sometimes, he wonders how much dimethylnitrosamine Steve stole and what became of the unused portion.
- Douglas County Chief Public Defender Lawrence J. Corrigan is a Douglas County District Court judge.
- Dr. Renate Kimbrough quit her job at CDC. Now she works for the Institute for Evaluating Health Risks, a private company.
- On occasion, Kimbrough has written letters to the surviving victims, recommending regular examinations for cancer

growth and asking for permission to follow their health. But she has never mailed them. Explained Kimbrough: "I did not want to upset them anymore. I decided it was not worth upsetting them for scientific reasons."

- Dr. Werner U. Spitz retired as a medical examiner in 1988. As a private expert witness, he testified for the prosecution in the New York "preppy murder" trial of Robert Chambers.

- After his failed marriage to Sandy, his high-school sweetheart, Jim Murphy headed to Peoria, Illinois, to manage a large restaurant. He knew nothing of the poisonings until he returned to his hometown after the trial.

- Through all the years of wandering around the country, and a second marriage that ended in divorce in 1986, Murphy saved two sets of engagement-wedding rings that Sandy tried to destroy. Every time the price of silver goes up, he thinks of melting them down and making a few bucks. But he doesn't. They remind him too much of "a nutty relationship with the petite blonde" he once loved.